DINOSAUR BAKE

POLYMER CLAY

POLYMER CLAY

Sculpt 10 Colorful Dinosaurs with Polymer Clay

Joan Cabarrus

JFCRN

DINOSAUR BAKE
POLYMER CLAY

Published in the United States of America in 2024 by JFCRN Publications.

Edited by Kristin Gilger.

Front and back cover pages, illustrations, photos, and book designed by Joan Cabarrus.

Sculpey® product photos provided by Polyform Products.

Library of Congress Control Number: 2024911731

ISBN: 979-8-9890295-0-1 (Paperback)

Printed in United States of America

First printing edition 2024
1 2 3 4 5 6 7 8 9 10

www.JFCRN.com

CONTENTS

Dinosaur Projects

The projects in this book require the use of a conventional or toaster oven and sharp tools. Adult supervision is advised.

Some projects require a few clay parts to be baked before adding them to the sculpture. The preparation pages will specify which clay parts should be baked beforehand and what tools are needed for each sculpture. Strictly follow the directions on each page.

You will use two different types of SCULPEY polymer clay to be blended together.

The sizes of the clay parts on the preparation page are approximately the sizes you'll be making to create your sculptures. Use the preparation page as a guide. Some of the clay shape labels on the preparation page are general terms used only for the purpose of this book; for example, a clay part may be described as a "back spot" to describe a different color spot on the dinosaur's skin. This is done for the sake of simplicity.

For each project, look for the colored block to the left side of the dinosaur's name. This color indicates the project's level of difficulty.

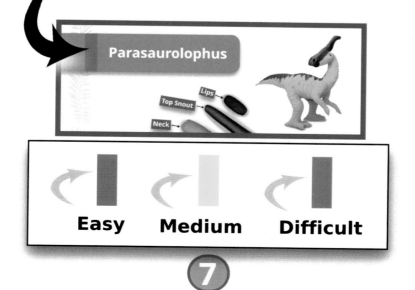

Easy   Medium   Difficult

MATERIALS

In this book, you will learn how to create full-figure dinosaur sculptures using select tools, DIY tools for skin texturing, clay, and your hands. Polymer clay is highly recommended to preserve the quality and stability of the sculptures. An oven is required.

POLYMER CLAY

Sculpey original in Terra Cotta and Sculpey III

Polymer clay is made of plastic and some fillers. It hardens only when baked at the right temperature and time in an oven. You will need one Sculpey III® 30 Color Sampler (1.88 lb/853 g) and four Original Sculpey® (1 lb/454 g) Terra Cotta color. Mixing the Terra Cotta clay with the colored clay will slightly lessen the vibrancy of the colors, making the dinosaur sculptures look more natural.

Sculpey Oven-Bake Clay Adhesive

Sculpey Oven-Bake Clay Adhesive (2 oz) will be used to secure select dinosaurs' spikes and spines to the body. It is also a good way to add more security between connecting parts and teeth or to fix breakages and cracks. This liquid is effective only when baked along with the sculpture.

Toaster oven for Baking

You will use a conventional or toaster oven to bake the sculptures. Make sure to test your oven and calibrate the temperature before baking a project.

Scissors

You will use scissors to trim toothpicks and cut pieces of card.

Toothpicks

You will use wooden toothpicks to create teeth for select dinosaurs. You will also use toothpicks to create stability, texture and score the clay, poke holes, and make indentations.

Construction Paper, Assorted Colors

You will use small pieces of card or construction paper to slice the clay and separate parts of the sculpture. You can use these card pieces instead of sharp tools when slicing is necessary.

Aluminum Foil

You will use aluminum foil as a platform, carrier, and stabilizer for the sculptures.

Baby oil and Soft-bristled Brush

You will use baby oil and a small soft-bristled brush to eliminate fingerprints and smooth out clay surfaces.

Ball Stylus Tool

You will need a small tipped ball stylus tool to create a Do-It-Yourself tool for skin texturing.

Do-It-Yourself

Texturing Tools

Mold for Dinosaur Skin Texturing

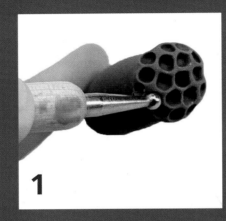
1

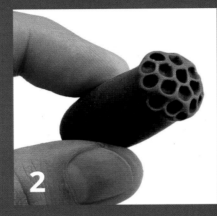
2

3

1 Form an oblong-shaped clay approximately 0.5 inch thick and 2 inches long. Take a small tipped ball stylus tool and press the tip deeply into the top of the clay. Cover the surface with holes.

2 Make sure to keep the top of the clay slightly curved and the holes evenly spaced.

3 Bake the clay mold in the toaster oven at 250°F for 20 minutes.

4 Let the clay mold cool off. Test the mold by pressing it on a piece of soft clay.

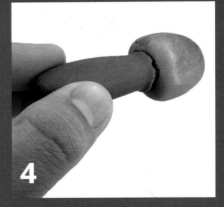
4

Toothpick for Texturing

1   Form the clay into the shape needed for the sculpture.

2   Score the clay with the toothpick, moving in one direction.

3   Smooth the clay with a soft-bristled brush and minimal amount of baby oil, brushing along the direction of the scored lines.

4   Another texturing technique is to draw lines with a toothpick; for example, to create the rough texture and pattern of dinosaur skin.

Learn the basic clay shapes before you begin to create your dinosaur sculptures. All you need to do is form several general shapes with clay then put them together.

Carrot and Cone Shapes

The carrot clay shape is long with one end thinner than the other. It will be used to create tails, horns, spikes, nails, and mouth parts. The cone shape is a shorter version of the carrot shape.

Ball Shape

The ball clay shape is spherical and will be used to create eyeballs, heads, and other body parts.

Irregular Log Shape

The irregular log shape is formed by connecting a few clay parts together.

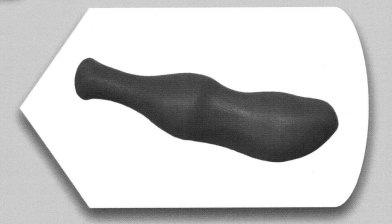

oblong Shape

The oblong clay shape is an elongated oval that will be used to form the body, body spots, neck, and head of the dinosaurs in this book. The shape and size will depend on how you roll the clay and if you flatten it.

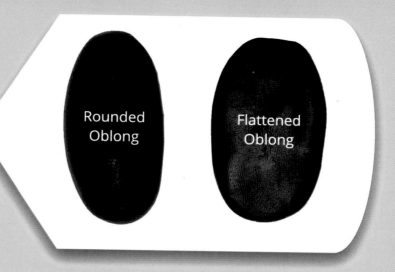

Rounded Oblong

Flattened Oblong

Diamond Shape

The diamond clay shape will be used to form the spines of the Stegosaurus. It may be formed with rounded or pointed ends.

Thin and Thick Log shapes

The log clay shape will be used to form the legs, tails, horns, spikes, and spots for select dinosaurs. Log shapes range from thin to thick depending on the clay part needed for the sculpture.

BASIC TECHNIQUES

Pinch

Pinching the clay is done by thinning a part of a clay with your fingertips. You will use this technique to combine layers of clay, create pointed tips, and thin body parts. The amount of pressure you use will depend on how thin or thick the clay part needs to be.

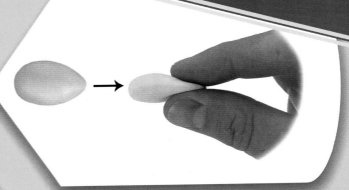

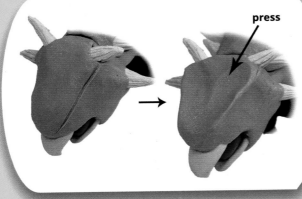

press

Fingertip Press

Pressing the clay is done by using your fingertip to create a crater-like indentation or to flatten a clay part. The dip can range from shallow to deep.

Rolling

The rolling technique is used to form the carrot and ball shapes. For the carrot shape, roll the clay back and forth against a hard, flat surface with your fingertips or palm. Next, put more pressure on one side of the clay while continuing to roll the clay to thin it. For the ball shape, roll the clay in a circular motion, using your fingertips when creating a small piece and your palm when creating a larger piece.

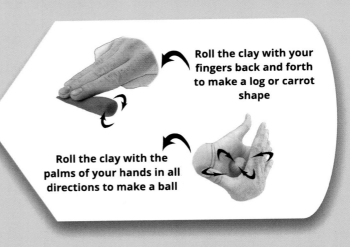

Roll the clay with your fingers back and forth to make a log or carrot shape

Roll the clay with the palms of your hands in all directions to make a ball

14

Flatten

Your fingertips or palms will be used to flatten small pieces of clay by pressing the clay on a hard, flat surface. Flattened clay will be used to form the spots of select creatures.

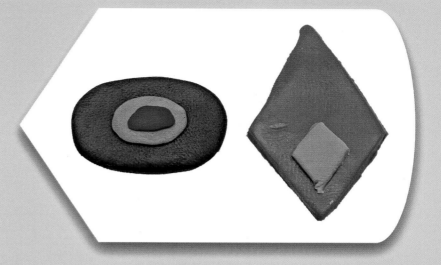

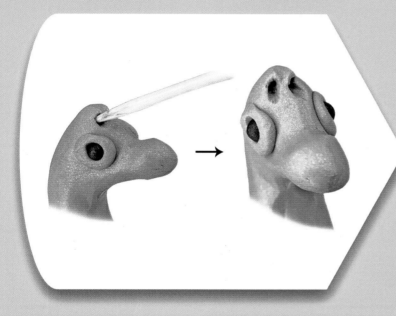

Poke

The poking technique is done by using a tool to create indentations on the surface of the clay and can be done with either light or hard pressure. You will use a toothpick to poke small holes to create a dinosaur's nostrils.

Score

Scoring is done by using a toothpick to create lines on the surface of the clay. You will use this technique to texture the skin and horns of a dinosaur. You will apply deeper pressure on thick clay and lighter pressure on thin clay.

Color Layering

Color layering is done by adding one or more differently colored pieces of clay on top of a shaped clay. This includes adding colored spots to a sculpture.

Mixing

Before blending differently colored pieces of clay, it is important to first wash your fingertips and hands. Avoid exposing your workspace to lint, dust, or animal fur. Condition or warm Sculpey III and Original Sculpey Terra Cotta with a warm wash cloth to soften the clay before using it. Evenly blending several colors of polymer clay will help you achieve the preferred color for your dinosaur sculptures.

clay + clay → =

Smearing

The smearing technique is used to create gradients of color on the surface of the sculpture. Smearing transitions the clay color from dark to light and vice versa. You will use your fingertips to slowly smear just the very edge or tip of one clay to another repeatedly.

Card Piece for Slicing

You will use the edge of a card or piece of construction paper to create separation for the mouth, fingers, toes, and other parts of the dinosaur. This is a safer alternative than using sharp tools like crafting knifes.

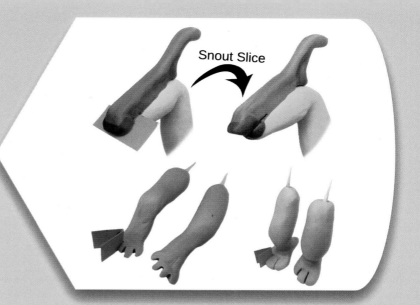

Snout Slice

Toothpick Teeth

You will use toothpicks to create teeth for the Tyrannosaurus Rex, Carcharodontosaurus, Suchomimus, and Dilophosaurus. This is done by trimming the very small part of the toothpick tips then inserting them into the clay. If necessary, you can secure them further with Sculpey Oven-Bake Clay Adhesive.

Toothpick Skewers

You will use toothpicks to connect large pieces of clay and create stability on select body parts. Trim the toothpicks by cutting them with scissors. Make sure that the tip that will connect to the body is long enough to create stability but not long enough to be exposed. Use longer toothpicks to connect the heads of dinosaurs with longer necks.

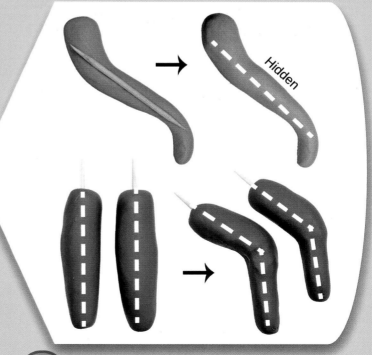

Hidden

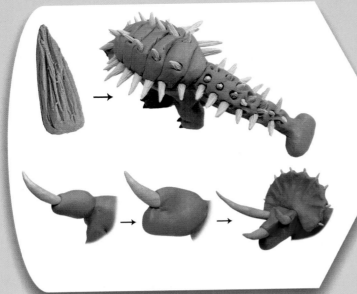

Shaping the Horns and Spikes

You will form the horns and spikes and bake them before adding them to the sculpture. Some dinosaurs will have very pointed spikes, and some will have rounded tips.

Shaping the Legs and Claws

After you attach and blend the connections between the legs and the body, you will use the pinching technique to form the knees, elbows, hands, and feet of select dinosaurs.

For other dinosaurs that require the hind legs to be baked before adding them to the sculpture, you will use the pinching technique to form the hands and feet. You will then use a piece of card to slice and form the toes and fingers.

The baked nails will be added to each fingertip and toe.

You will texture each hind leg with a toothpick then smooth the surface with a brush and baby oil.

Make sure that the hind legs are upright and stable before baking them in the oven.

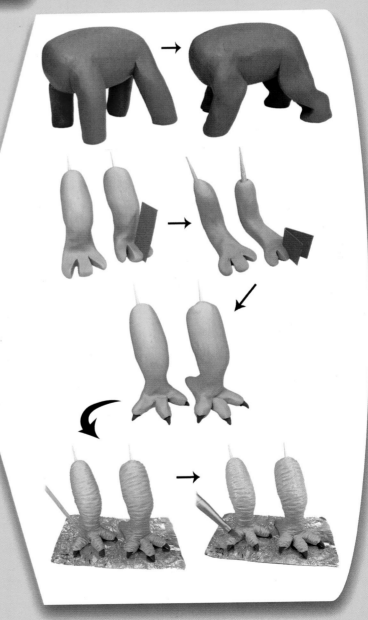

Smoothing and Removing Fingerprints

Since you will be touching and holding the sculptures, your fingers will leave prints. You can use a soft-bristled brush and a drop of baby oil to help smooth and remove fingerprints and any excess clay after texturing. Do this right before baking, when the sculpture is on the baking sheet.

Baked Clay on Soft Clay

You will bake the eyeballs, horns, nails, and spikes before adding them to the sculpture. This will preserve the color and shape of the baked clay parts while you continue to form the rest of the sculpture.

Sculpey Oven-Bake Adhesive will help adhere the baked clay to the soft clay. This is only effective when baked in the oven. Follow the product package insert for directions.

You will bake the small pieces of clay at 250°F for 2 minutes. Make sure that your pieces are securely situated inside the oven and do not touch any of the oven surfaces.

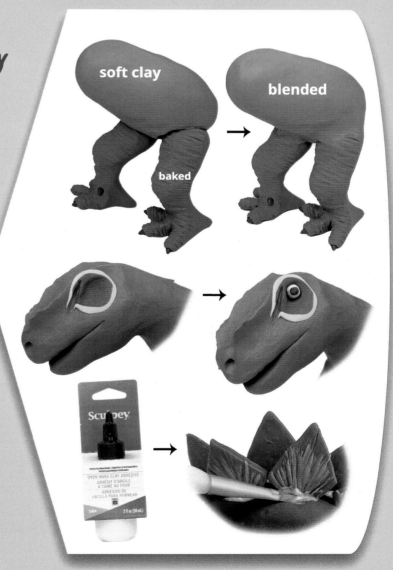

Preparing to Bake

For dinosaurs that are standing on two feet, like the Dilophosaurus or Tyrannosaurus Rex, widen the base of the baked legs. Adjust the head positioning and the tail for balance, and prop the sculpture upright with extra aluminum foil to create stability before baking. Polymer clay softens in the oven when it is hot, so there is a risk of some thin parts breaking. If the sculpture is imbalanced after baking, add little pieces of clay underneath the feet to re-balance the weight then re-bake the piece.

Baking the Sculpture in an Oven

Make sure to test your oven and calibrate the temperature before baking a project. You will bake whole sculptures at 250°F for 20 minutes. Very small and very thin pieces will be baked for 1-2 minutes. Make sure that your aluminum foil platform is flat.

Make sure the sculpture does not touch any heating elements in the oven to prevent scorching or burning.

Fixing Cracks or Breakage

Cracks in a sculpture can occur during baking, and breakages can result from mishandling. In such cases, use Sculpey Oven-Bake Clay Adhesive to re-attach the broken pieces and then re-bake the piece according to the package insert or at 250°F for 30 minutes.

10

Dinosaur Projects

Parasaurolophus

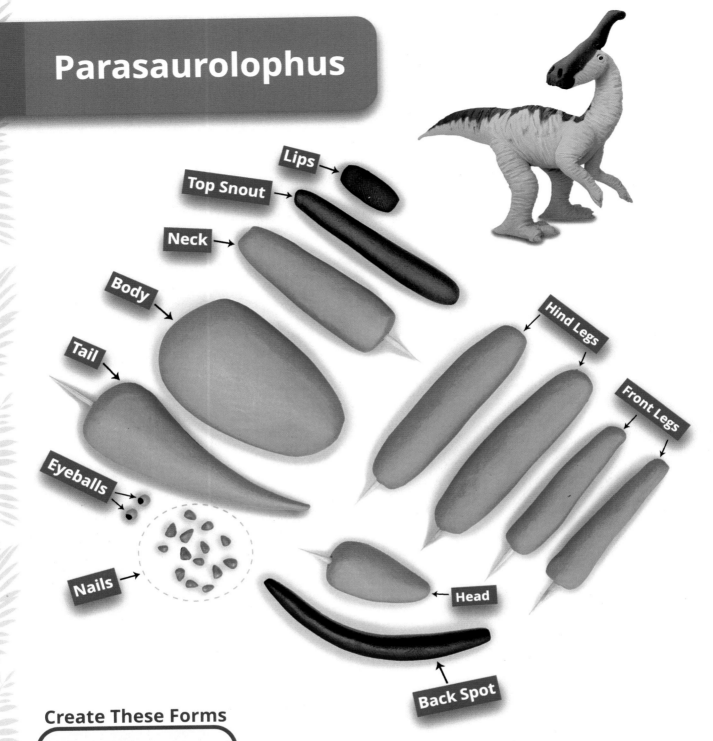

Labels on parts: Lips, Top Snout, Neck, Body, Tail, Eyeballs, Nails, Hind Legs, Front Legs, Head, Back Spot

Create These Forms

You will bake the eyeballs and nails for 2 minutes at 250°F before adding them to the sculpture. Strictly follow the instructions on the next page.

TOOLS NEEDED:

- Toothpicks

- Scissors

- Pieces of card

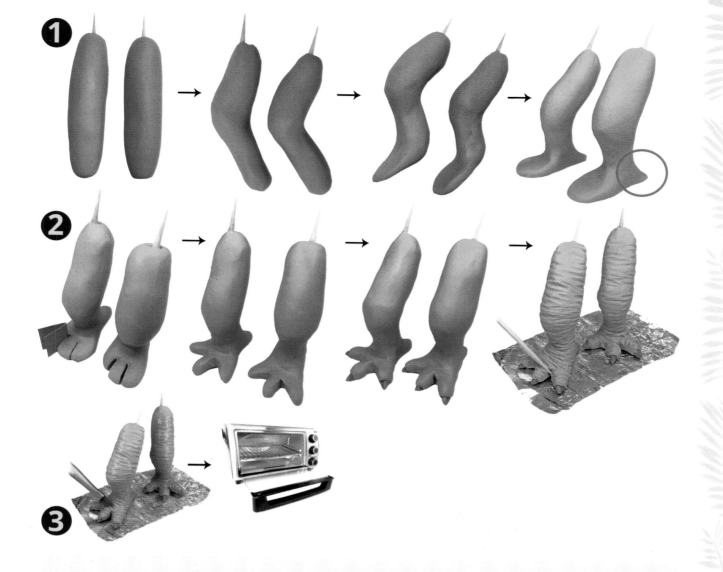

1 Prepare the skewered hind legs clay. Bend the clay and skewer at the midpoint of each leg. This will break the toothpick inside. Pinch the end tips of the legs to create the feet formations. Pinch the back of both feet to create a heel for stability.

2 Use a piece of card to slice two evenly spaced lines. This will create three toes on each foot. Separate and form the individual toes slightly pointed. Add the baked nails to the tip of each toe.

Using a toothpick, texture the legs with horizontal indentations.

3 Place the hind legs on an aluminum platform then smooth the surface of the clay with a brush and small amount of baby oil. Make sure that both legs are upright. Bake the legs at 250°F for 20 minutes.

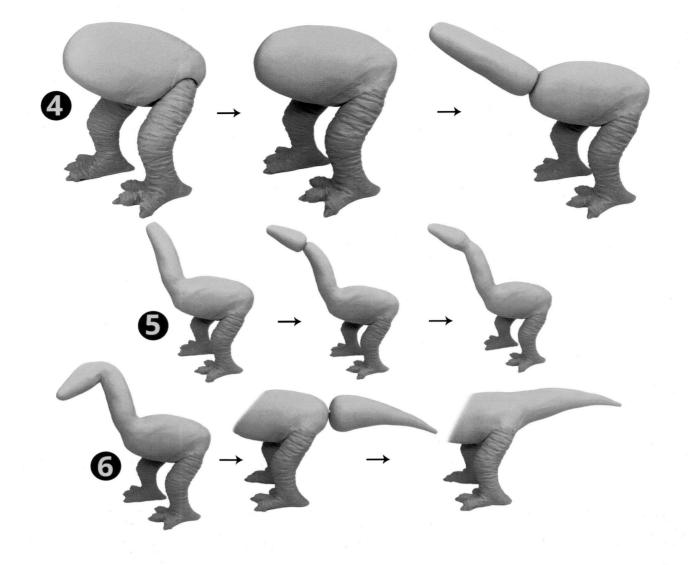

4 After the baked hind legs cool off, attach them to the body. Blend the connections, smoothing the soft clay towards the baked clay.

Attach the neck.

5 Blend the connection between the neck and body. Attach the head to the tip of the neck then blend the connection.

6 Bend the head slightly downwards.

Attach the tail then blend the connection.

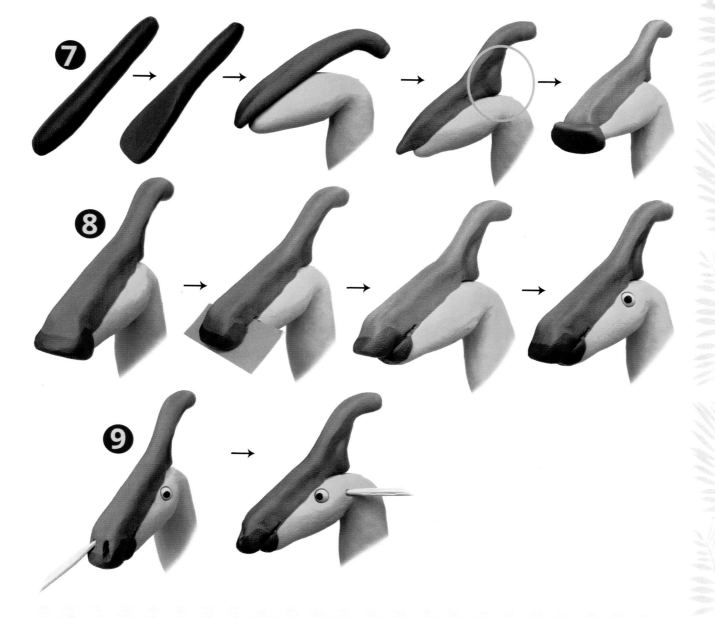

7 Prepare the top snout. Lightly pinch one end of the top snout clay to create the front part of the snout. Attach the top snout to the head, aligning the pinched end with the mouth area. Lightly press the edges of the top snout onto the head then pinch the clay at the lower back of the top snout.

Add the lips horizontally to the front of the mouth.

8 Connect the lips to the top snout by lightly pressing down on the edges.

Slice the mouth horizontally with a piece of card. Shorten the bottom mouth by lightly pressing it inward.

Add the baked eyeballs to each side of the head.

9 Using a toothpick, poke two holes into the top front of the snout to create nostrils. Poke one hole into each side of the head to create ear holes.

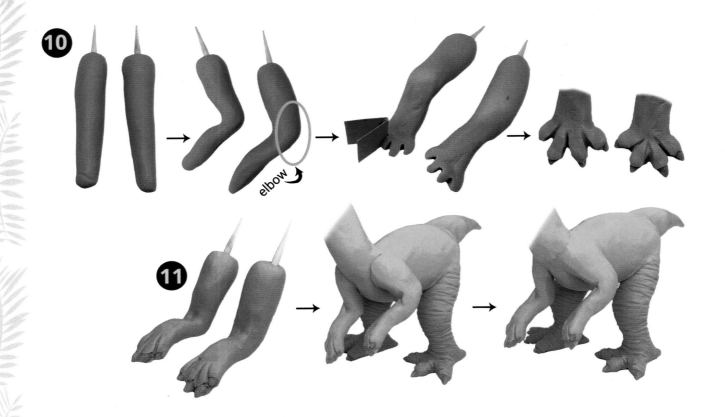

10 Prepare the skewered front legs. Bend both the clay and skewer at the midpoint of each front leg. This will break the toothpick inside and create an elbow.

Pinch the end tips of the front legs to create the hand formations. Use a piece of card to slice three evenly spaced lines. This will create four fingers on each hand. Add the baked nails to the tip of each finger then deepen the separation of the individual fingers with a piece of card.

11 Attach the front leg formations to each side of the shoulder area then blend the connections.

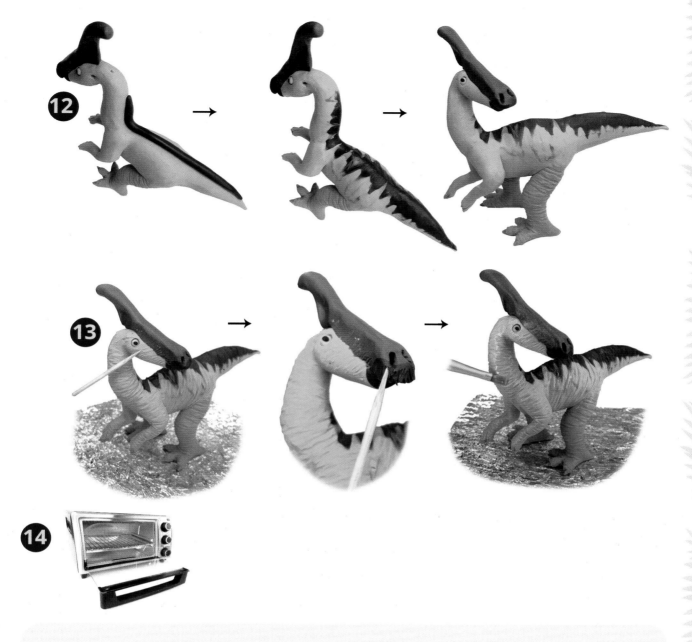

12 Add the back spot, aligning it with the spine of the dinosaur. Smear the sides of the back spot downwards then smear the yellow clay from the body upwards to create an irregular zigzag pattern.

Maneuver the head to face sideways.

13 Place the sculpture on an aluminum platform.

Texture the body, face, head, and lips with a toothpick.

Smooth the surface of the sculpture with a brush and small amount of baby oil.

14 Bake the sculpture at 250°F for 20 minutes.

Carcharodontosaurus

Back Spot

Spikes

Tail

Eye Spots

Eyeballs

Teeth

Front Legs

Hind Legs

Head

Neck

Nails

Body

Create These Forms

You will bake the eyeballs and nails for 2 minutes at 250°F before adding them to the sculpture. You will also cut the small tips of naturally colored wooden toothpicks to create the teeth. Strictly follow the instructions on the next page.

TOOLS NEEDED:

- Toothpicks

- Scissors

- Pieces of card

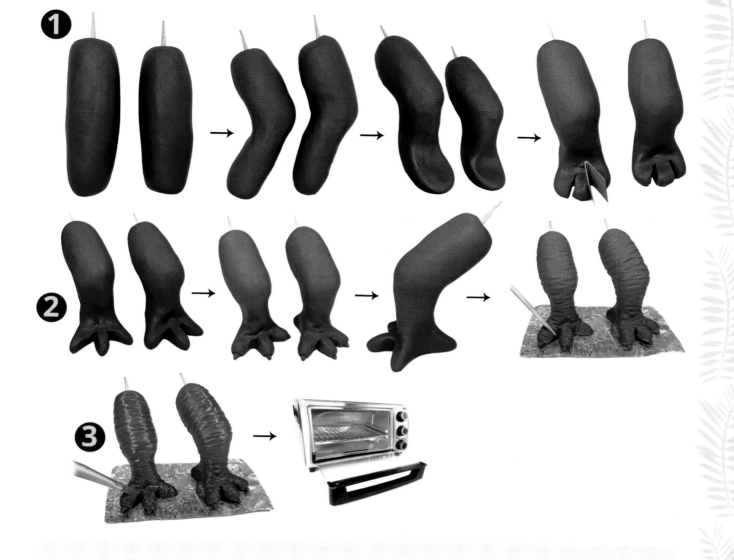

1 Prepare the skewered hind legs clay. Bend the clay and skewer at the midpoint of each leg. This will break the toothpick inside. Pinch the end tips of the legs to create the feet formations. Use a piece of card to slice two evenly spaced lines. This will create three toes for each foot.

2 Separate then form the individual toes slightly pointed. Add the baked nails to the tip of each toe. Pinch the back of both feet to create a heel for stability.

Place the hind leg formations on an aluminum platform. Using a toothpick, texture the legs with horizontal indentations.

3 Place the hind legs on an aluminum platform then smooth the surface with a brush and small amount of baby oil. Make sure that both legs are upright. Bake the sculpture at 250°F for 20 minutes.

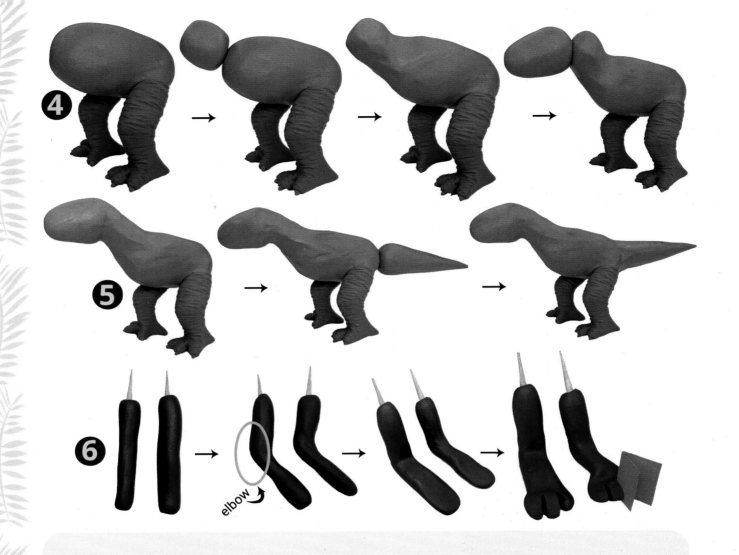

4 After the baked hind legs cool off, attach them to the body. Blend the connections, smoothing the soft clay towards the baked clay.

Attach the neck then blend the connection.

Attach the head to the front of the neck.

5 Blend the connection between the head and neck.

Attach the tail then blend the connection.

6 Prepare the skewered front legs. Bend both the clay and skewer at the midpoint of each leg. This will break the toothpick inside and create an elbow.

Pinch the end tips of the front legs to create the hand formations. Use a piece of card to slice two evenly spaced lines. This will create three fingers on each hand.

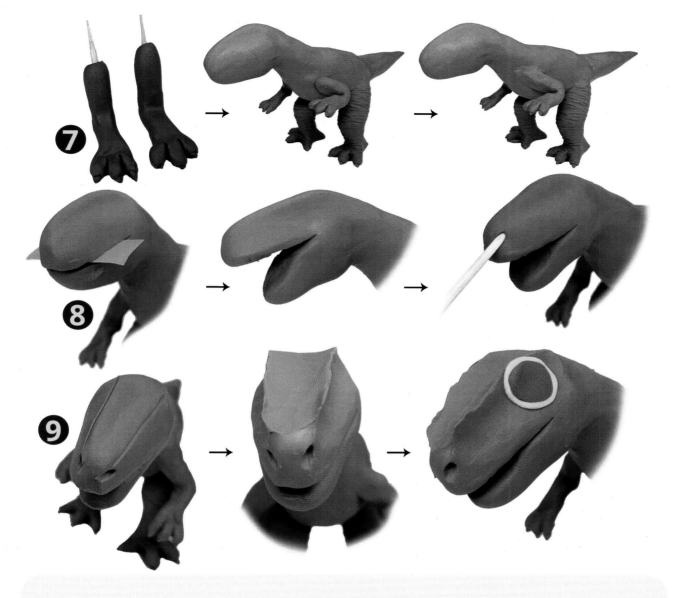

7 Add the baked nails to the tip of each finger.

Attach the front leg formations to each side of the shoulder area then blend the connections.

8 Deeply slice the mouth horizontally with a piece of card then open the mouth.

Using a toothpick, poke two holes into the top front of the snout to create nostrils.

9 Using a toothpick, draw two parallel lines on top of the head, starting at the nostrils and moving towards the back of the head. Gently pinch the lines to create two parallel raised crests.

Place the eye spots on both sides of the head.

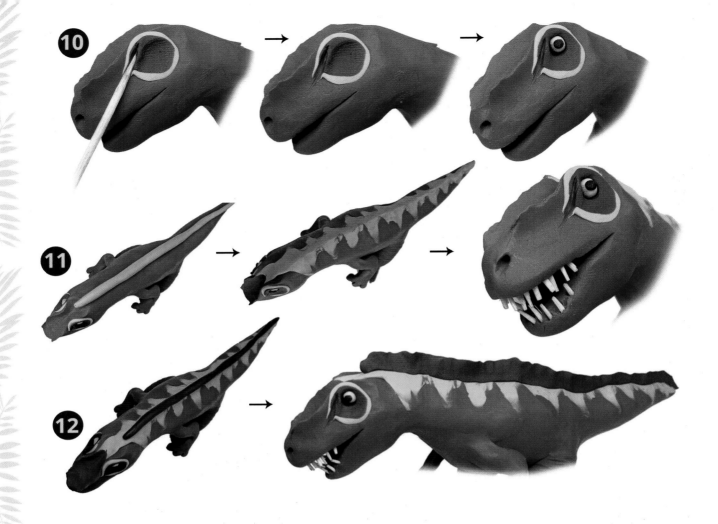

10 Using a toothpick, score a line downward at the front of each eye spot. Add the baked eyeballs to the eye spots.

11 Add the back spot, aligning it with the spine of the dinosaur. Smear the sides of the back spot downwards then smear the maroon clay from the body upwards to create an irregular zigzag pattern.

Add the teeth on the inner edges of the lower and upper mouth.

12 Add the spike clay on the back, aligning it with the body spot. Pinch the spike clay upward.

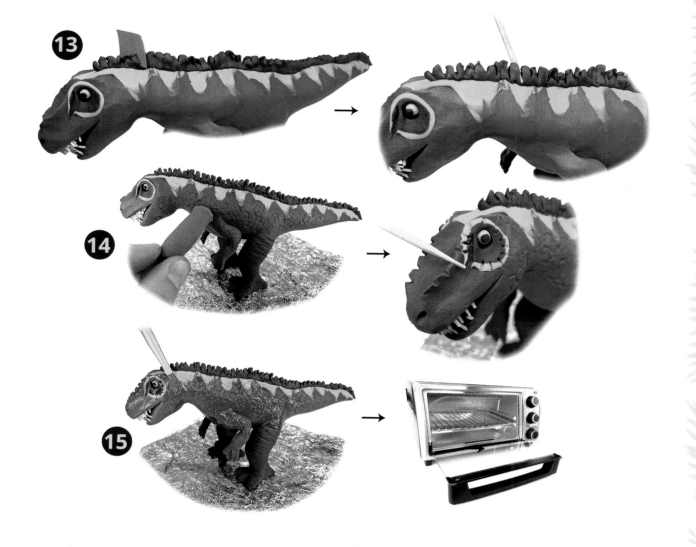

13 Using a piece of card, slice the spike clay to create the individual spikes. Use a toothpick to further shape and separate the spikes.

14 Use your Do-It-Yourself skin texturing tool to texture the body.

Use a toothpick to create indentations on the raised crests on the snout and the edges of the eye spots.

15 Place the sculpture on an aluminum platform then smooth the surface with a brush and small amount of baby oil.

Bake the sculpture at 250°F for 20 minutes.

Regaliceratops

Create These Forms

You will bake the eyeballs, nails, and horns for 2 minutes at 250°F before adding them to the sculpture. You will also cut the small tips of naturally colored wooden toothpicks to create the teeth. Strictly follow the instructions on the next page.

TOOLS NEEDED:

- Toothpicks
- Scissors
- Pieces of card

Front Horn

Long Horns

Eyeballs

Spikes

Nails

Front Legs

Neck

Head

Hind Legs

Upper Beak

Frill Spots

Lower Beak

Cheek Flaps

Body

Eyes

Back Spot

Frills

Tail

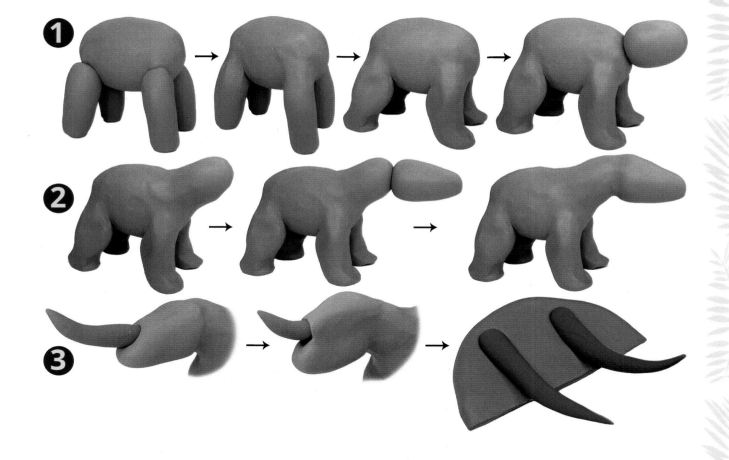

1 Attach the front legs and hind legs to the body then blend the connections. Lightly pinch the midpoint of each leg to create knees and elbows. Lightly pinch the endpoint of each leg to create feet.

Attach the neck.

2 Blend the connection between the neck and body.

Attach the head to the front of the neck then blend the connection.

3 Insert the baked front horn into the middle of the top of the snout. Make sure that the front tip of the horn is pointing upward. Gently press the horn until about half its length is inside the snout clay. Form the snout under the horn.

Place and lightly depress the two baked long horns parallel to each other on top of one frill clay. Make sure that the tips of the horns are pointing upward.

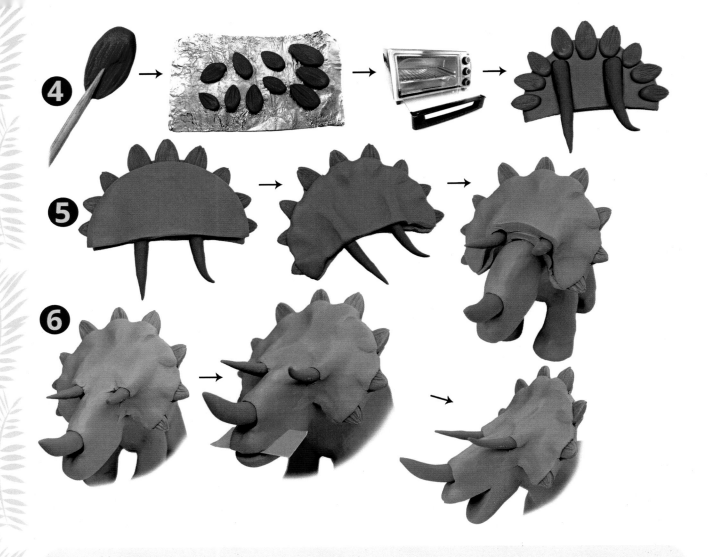

4 Texture each spike with a toothpick. Place the spikes on an aluminum platform and bake at 250°F for 2 minutes.

After the spikes cool off, place the spikes along the round edge of the frill, making sure that only the bottom half of each spike touches the frill clay. Make sure that the spikes are pointing outward.

5 Place the second frill clay on top of the frill formation, covering the spikes and horns. Lightly press the frill to attach the pieces. You should be able to see the outline of the spikes and horns underneath. Place the newly formed frill on top of the head with the spikes pointing upward and the two long horns pointing forward.

6 Blend the connection between the frill and head.

Slice the mouth horizontally with a piece of card then open the mouth.

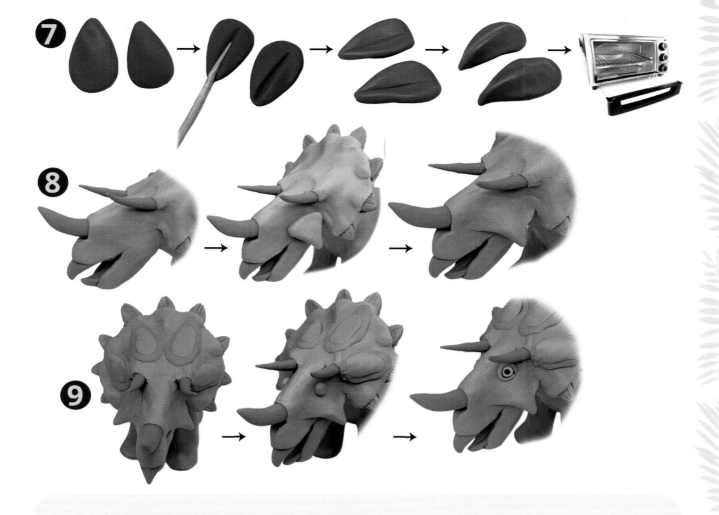

7 Prepare the upper and lower beak. Using a toothpick, create an indentation on each beak then slightly fold the beak towards the indentation. Turn the beaks over then pinch the midline of each beak.

Bake the beaks at 250°F for 2 minutes.

8 After the baked beaks cool off, place the baked upper beak on the inner part of the upper mouth pointing downwards. Place the baked lower beak on the inner part of the lower mouth pointing upwards. Make sure that the lower beak is shorter than the upper beak.

Place the cheek flaps on the sides of the head under the long horns pointing downward. Blend the connections between the cheek flaps and face.

9 Place the frill spots on the front of the frill.

Add the eyes right below the long horns.

Add and depress the baked eyeballs in each eye.

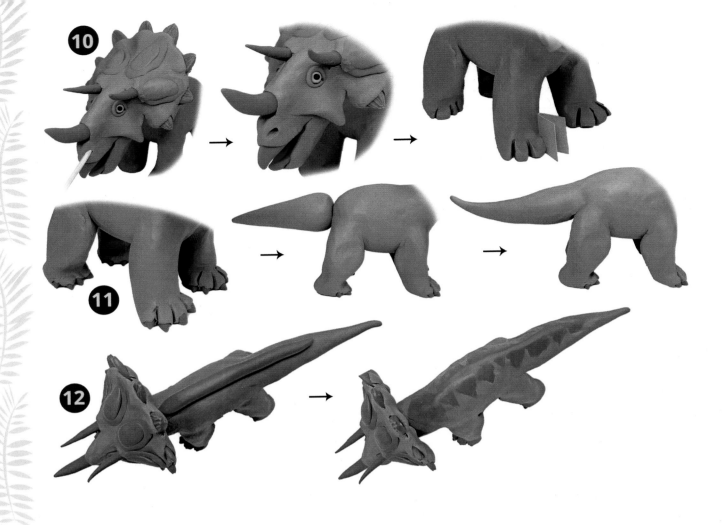

10 Using a toothpick, poke two holes in the front of the snout to form nostrils.

Use a piece of card to slice four evenly spaced lines in each foot. This will create five toes for each foot.

11 Add the baked nails to the tip of each toe.

Attach the tail then blend the connection.

12 Add the back spot, aligning it with the spine of the dinosaur. Smear the sides of the back spot downwards then smear the brown clay from the body upwards to create an irregular zigzag pattern.

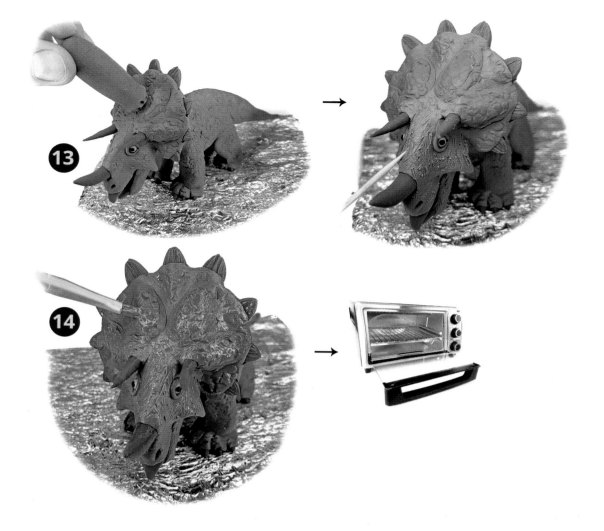

13 Place the sculpture on an aluminum platform. Use your Do-It-Yourself skin texturing tool to texture the body. Texture the head, face, and the legs by scoring the clay with a toothpick.

14 Smooth the surface with a brush and small amount of baby oil.

Bake the sculpture at 250°F for 20 minutes.

Tyrannosaurus Rex

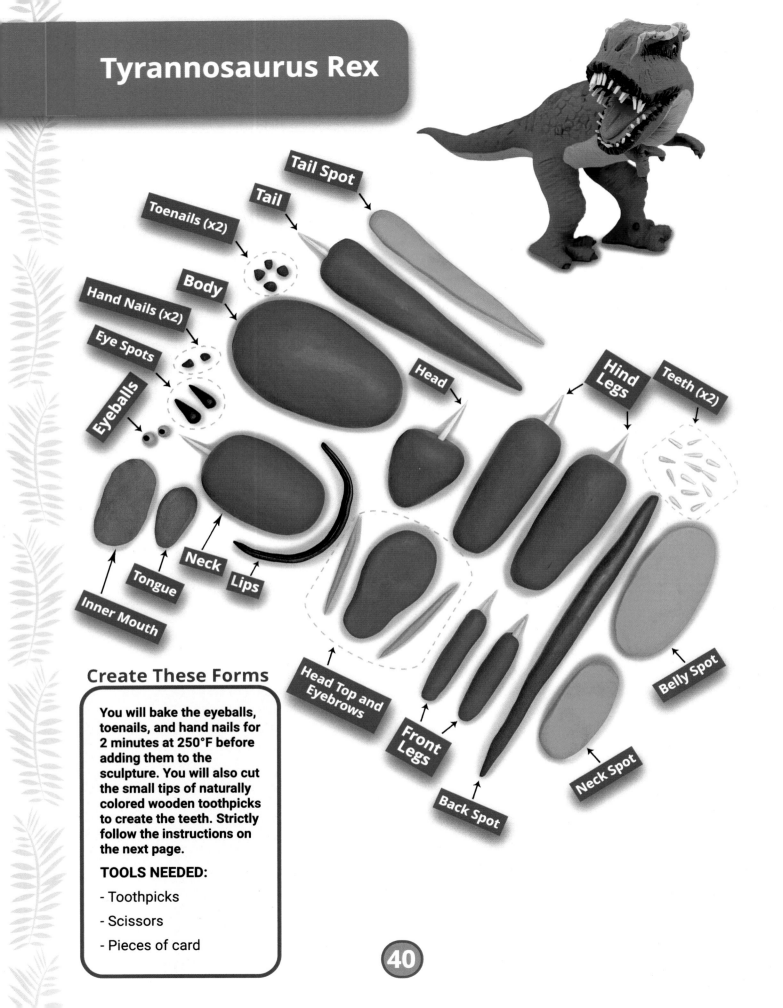

Tail Spot

Tail

Toenails (x2)

Body

Hand Nails (x2)

Eye Spots

Eyeballs

Head

Hind Legs

Teeth (x2)

Neck

Lips

Tongue

Inner Mouth

Head Top and Eyebrows

Front Legs

Back Spot

Neck Spot

Belly Spot

Create These Forms

You will bake the eyeballs, toenails, and hand nails for 2 minutes at 250°F before adding them to the sculpture. You will also cut the small tips of naturally colored wooden toothpicks to create the teeth. Strictly follow the instructions on the next page.

TOOLS NEEDED:

- Toothpicks

- Scissors

- Pieces of card

40

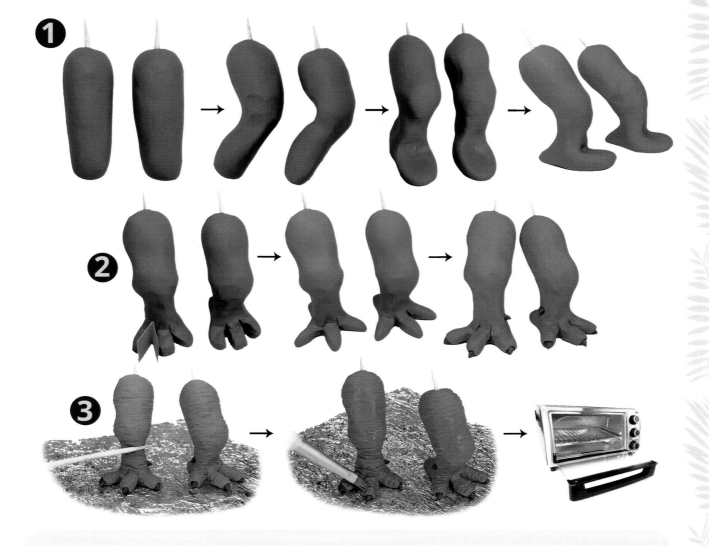

1 Prepare the skewered hind legs clay. Bend the clay and skewer at the midpoint of each hind leg. This will break the toothpick inside. Pinch the end tips of the legs to create the feet formations. Pinch the back of both feet to create a heel for stability.

2 Use a piece of card to slice two evenly spaced lines. This will create three toes on each foot. Separate and form the individual toes slightly pointed. Add the baked toenails to the tip of each toe and the heel.

3 Place the hind legs on an aluminum platform. Using a toothpick, texture the legs with horizontal indentations. Smooth the surface with a brush and small amount of baby oil. Make sure that both legs are upright. Bake the sculpture at 250°F for 20 minutes.

4 After the baked hind legs cool off, attach them to the body. Blend the connections, smoothing the soft clay towards the baked clay.

Attach the neck then blend the connection.

5 Attach the head to the tip of the neck then blend the connection. Maneuver the head to face sideways.

6 Attach the tail then blend the connection.

Place the belly spot along the belly area, the neck spot along the front neck area, and the tail spot underneath the tail.

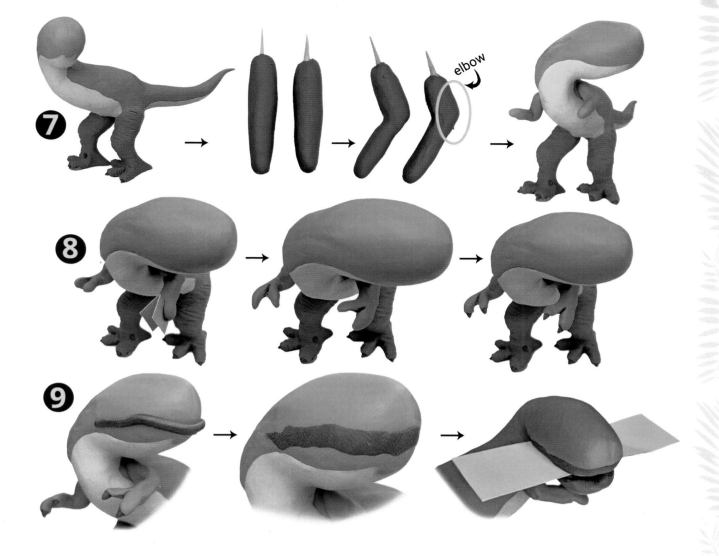

7 Lightly press and smear the edges of the neck, belly, and tail spots toward the body. Prepare the skewered front legs. Bend the clay and skewer at the midpoint of each leg. This will break the toothpick inside. Attach the front legs to each side of the shoulder area then blend the connections.

8 Use a piece of card to slice one line in the middle of each hand. This will create two fingers for each hand. Separate the fingers then add the baked hand nails to each fingertip.

9 Place the lips clay horizontally at the front of the face. Flatten the lips with your fingertip.

Deeply slice the lips and mouth in the middle horizontally with a large piece of card then open the mouth.

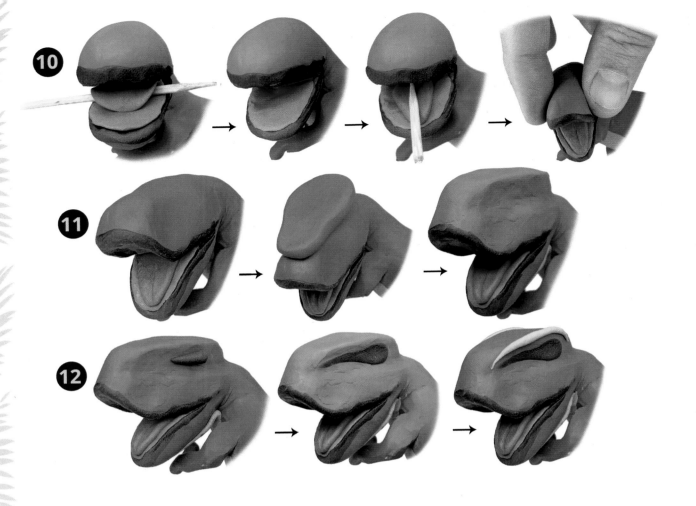

10

10 Use a toothpick to place the inner mouth clay inside the mouth.

Add the tongue then use a toothpick to create an indentation in the middle of the tongue.

Lightly pinch the top of the snout with your index finger and thumb.

11 Make sure that the sides of the top mouth are droopy.

Place the head top clay on top of the head then blend the connection. Make sure that the flat top stays flat.

12 Add the eye spots to each side of the head then lightly smear the front tip of each eye spot towards the front of the face.

Add the yellow eyebrows on top of each eye spot.

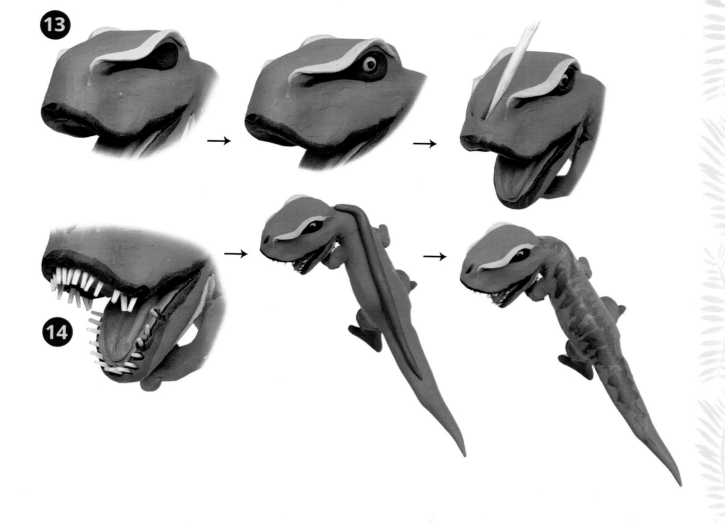

13   Pinch the eyebrows sideways.

Add and depress the eyeballs in each eye spot.

Using a toothpick, poke two holes at a slant in the front of the snout to create nostrils.

14   Add the teeth on the inner edges of the lower and upper mouth.

Add the back spot, aligning it with the spine of the dinosaur. Smear the sides of the back spot downwards then smear the green clay from the body upwards to create an irregular pattern.

15 Place the sculpture on an aluminum platform.

Use a toothpick to create slight indentations on the lips.

Use your Do-It-Yourself skin texturing tool to texture the body.

16 Using a toothpick, texture the skin of the face and legs by scoring the surface.

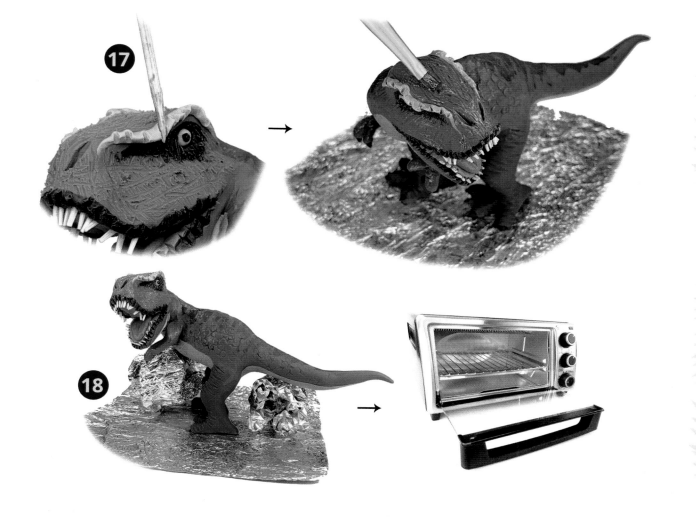

17 Create indentations on the eyebrows by lightly depressing a toothpick.

Smooth the surface of the sculpture with a brush and small amount of baby oil.

18 Prop the sculpture up by placing balls of aluminum foil underneath the tail and body. This will help stabilize the sculpture before baking.

Bake the sculpture at 250°F for 20 minutes.

Suchomimus

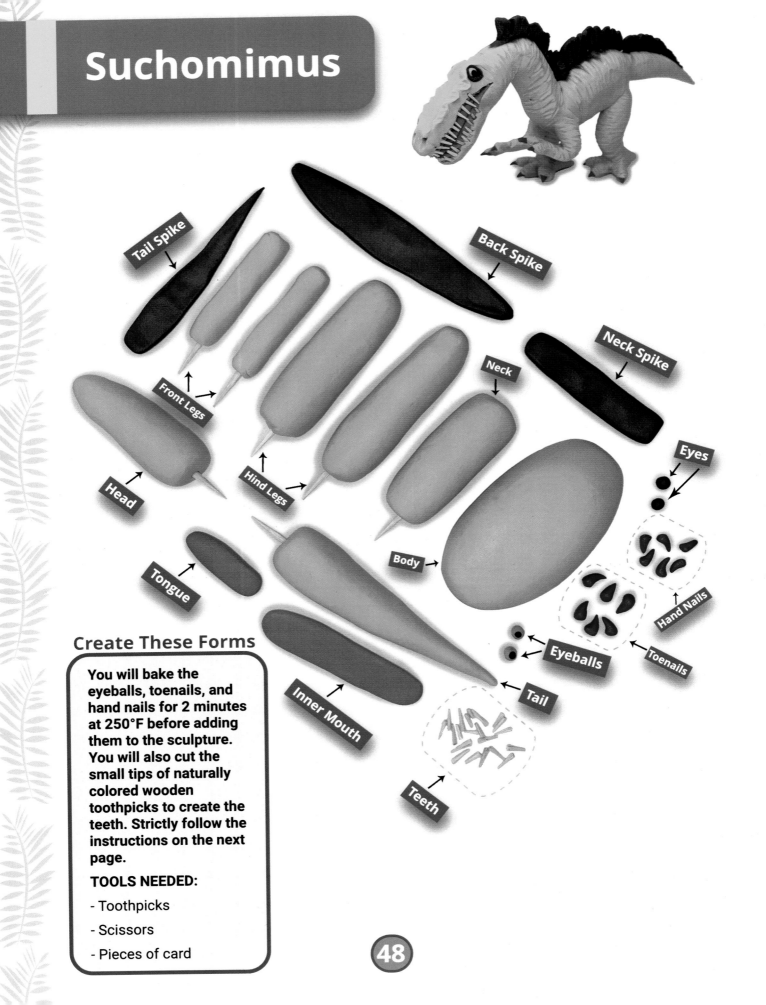

Tail Spike

Back Spike

Neck Spike

Front Legs

Neck

Head

Hind Legs

Eyes

Body

Tongue

Hand Nails

Eyeballs

Toenails

Inner Mouth

Tail

Teeth

Create These Forms

You will bake the eyeballs, toenails, and hand nails for 2 minutes at 250°F before adding them to the sculpture. You will also cut the small tips of naturally colored wooden toothpicks to create the teeth. Strictly follow the instructions on the next page.

TOOLS NEEDED:

- Toothpicks

- Scissors

- Pieces of card

48

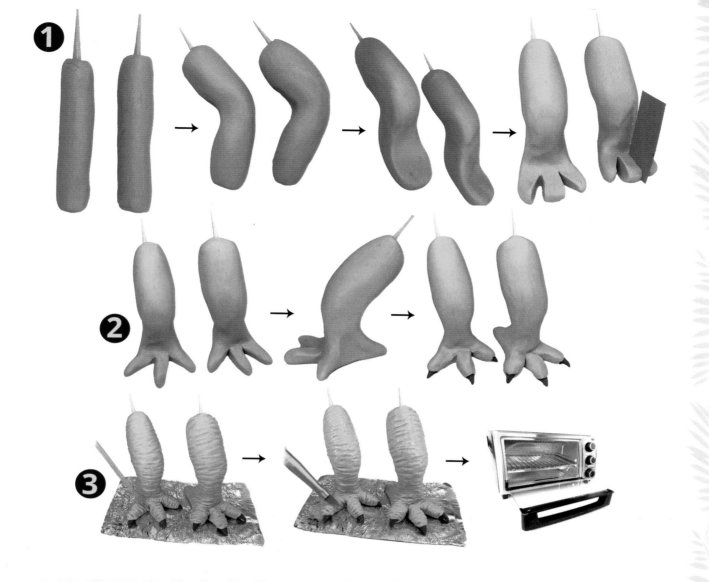

1 Prepare the skewered hind legs clay. Bend the clay and skewer at the midpoint of each leg. This will break the toothpick inside. Pinch the end tips of the legs to create the feet formations. Use a piece of card to slice two evenly separated lines. This will create three toes in each foot.

2 Separate and form the individual toes slightly pointed. Pinch the back of both feet to create a heel for stability.

Add the baked nails to the tip of each toe.

3 Place the hind legs on an aluminum platform. Using a toothpick, texture the legs with horizontal indentations. Smooth the surface with a brush and small amount of baby oil. Make sure that both legs are upright. Bake the sculpture at 250°F for 20 minutes.

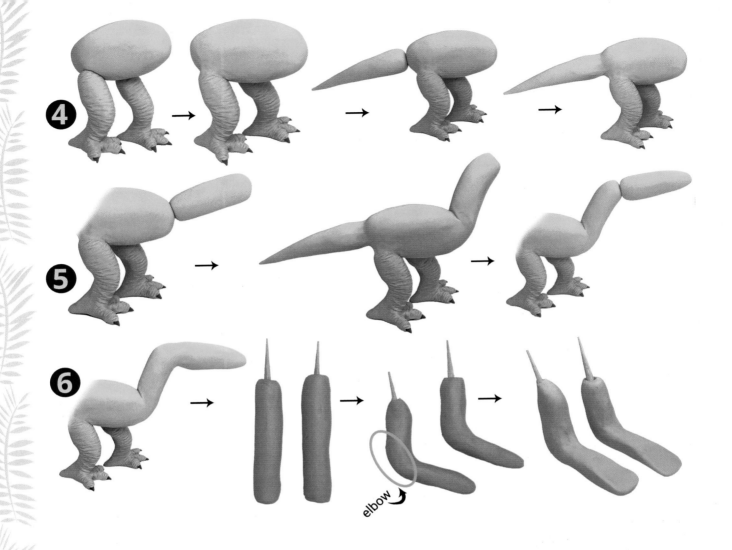

elbow

4 After the baked hind legs cool off, attach them to the body. Blend the connections, smoothing the soft clay towards the baked clay.

Attach the tail then blend the connection.

5 Attach the neck then blend the connection.

Attach the head to the front of the neck.

6 Blend the connection between the head and neck.

Prepare the skewered front legs. Bend both the clay and skewer at the midpoint of each front leg. This will break the toothpick inside and create an elbow.

Pinch the end tips of the front legs to create the hand formations.

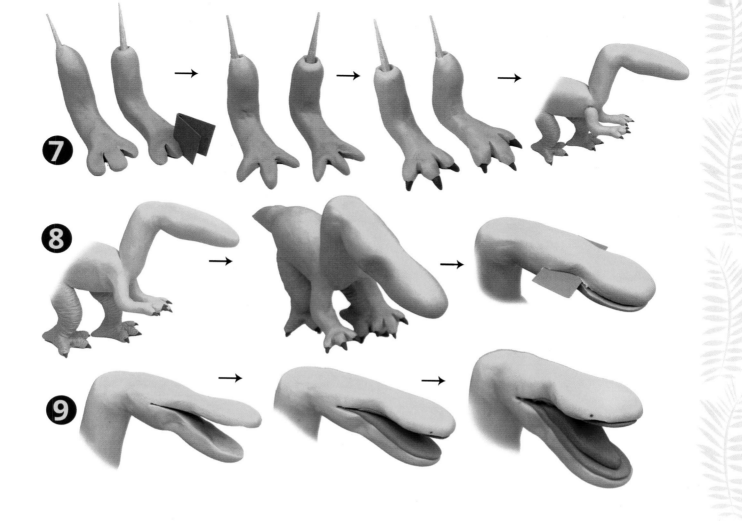

7 Use a piece of card to slice two evenly spaced lines. This will create three fingers on each hand.

Separate and form the individual fingers slightly pointed. Add the baked nails to the tip of each finger.

Attach the front leg formations to each side of the shoulder area.

8 Blend the connections between the front legs and body.

Lightly pinch the sides of the snout.

Deeply slice the middle of the snout horizontally with a piece of card to create a mouth.

9 Open the mouth then place the inner mouth clay inside.

Place the tongue inside the mouth.

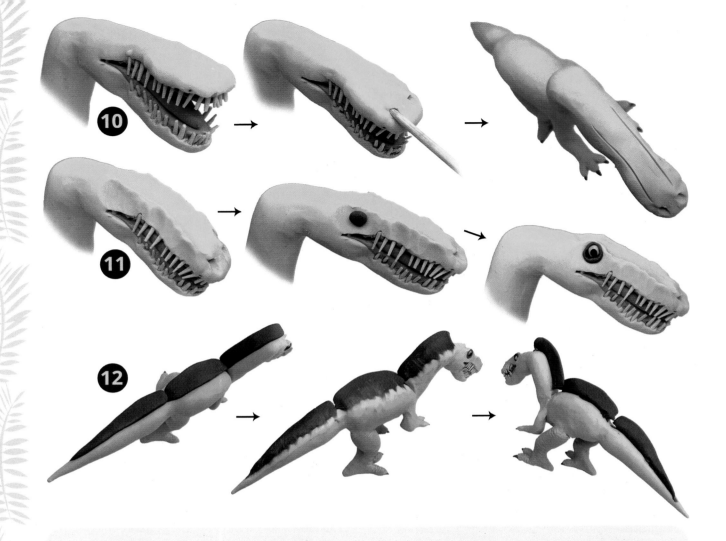

10 Add the teeth on the inner edges of the lower and upper mouth.

Poke two holes in the front of the snout to create nostrils.

11 Draw two parallel lines on top of the head, starting from the nostrils and moving towards the forehead.

Pinch the lines to create two parallel raised crests.

Add the eyes to each side of the head then add and depress the baked eyeballs on each eye.

12 Add the neck, back, and tail spikes along the spine of the dinosaur. Gently fold the spikes towards the left side then lightly smear the base of the right side downwards.

Gently lift up the spikes then smear the left side base of the spikes downwards.

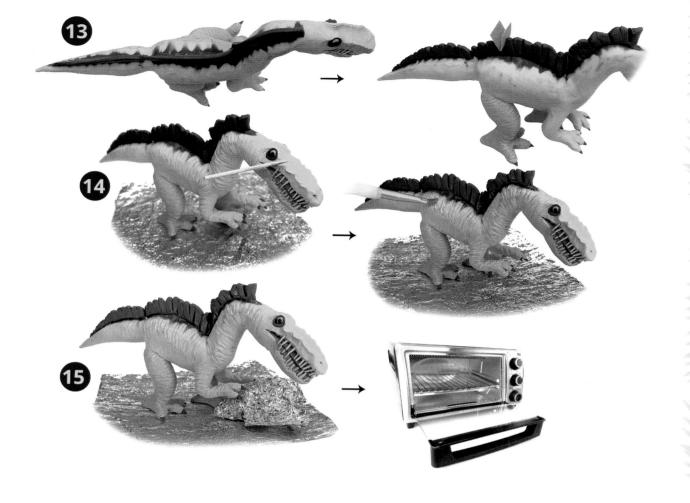

13 Slice the spike clay with a folded piece of card to create individual spikes.

14 Texture the head, face, body, tail, and front legs by scoring the clay with a toothpick.

Place the sculpture on an aluminum platform. Smooth the surface with a brush and small amount of baby oil.

15 Prop the sculpture up by placing balls of aluminum foil underneath the tail and body. This will help stabilize the sculpture before baking.

Bake the sculpture at 250°F for 20 minutes.

Brachiosaurus

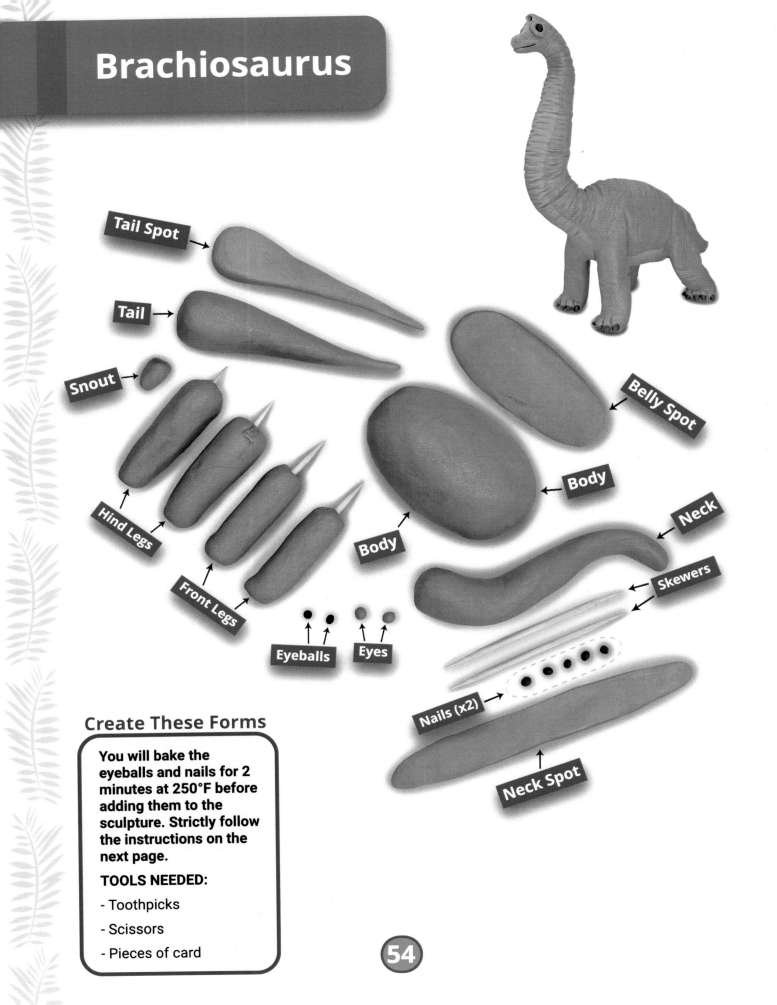

Tail Spot

Tail

Snout

Hind Legs

Front Legs

Body

Body

Belly Spot

Neck

Skewers

Eyeballs

Eyes

Nails (x2)

Neck Spot

Create These Forms

You will bake the eyeballs and nails for 2 minutes at 250°F before adding them to the sculpture. Strictly follow the instructions on the next page.

TOOLS NEEDED:

- Toothpicks

- Scissors

- Pieces of card

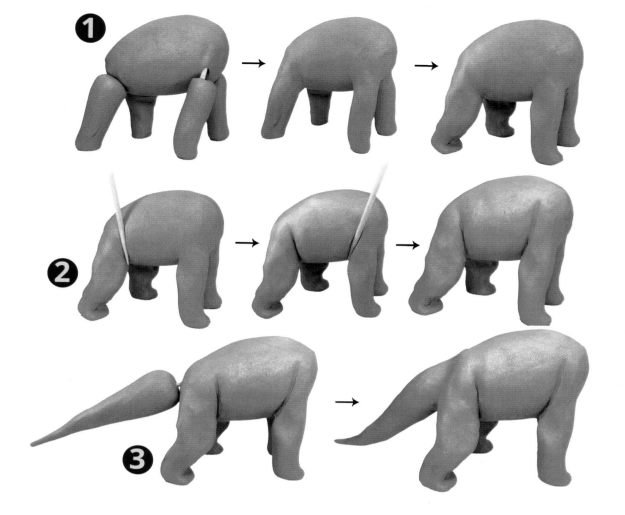

1   Attach the front and hind legs to the body then blend the connections. Lightly pinch the midpoint of each leg to create knees and elbows. Lightly pinch the endpoint of each leg to create feet.

2   Using a toothpick, create indentations where the front and hind legs meet the body.

3   Attach the tail then blend the connection.

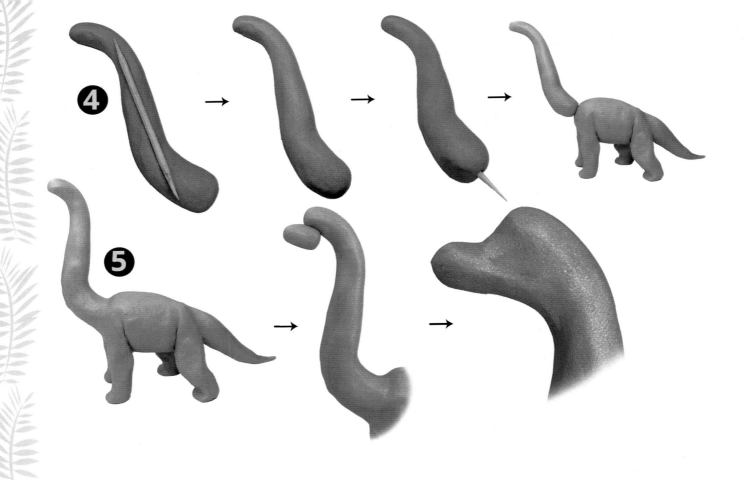

4 Place one toothpick skewer inside the neck clay. The skewer should not be visible.

Trim the second toothpick then attach it to the bottom tip of the neck clay. Attach the neck to the body.

5 Blend the connection between the neck and body.

Add the snout under the top tip of the neck then blend the connection.

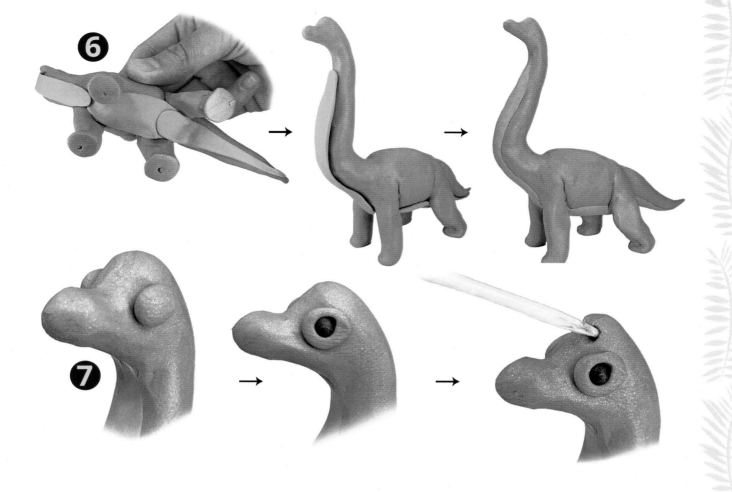

6 Place the belly spot along the belly area, the neck spot along the front neck area, and tail spot under the bottom tail area. Lightly press and flatten the edges of the spots with your fingertip.

7 Add the eyes to each side of the head.

Add and depress the baked eyeballs in each eye.

Light pinch the top part of the head to create a bump.

Using a toothpick, poke two holes in the front of the bump to create nostrils.

8 Use a folded piece of card to slice four evenly spaced lines in both the hands and feet. This will create five fingers on each hand and foot.

Add the baked nails to the tip of each finger and toe. Use the folded card to further define the separation between the fingers and toes.

9 Using a piece of card, slice the mouth horizontally then open the mouth.

Using a toothpick, texture the body, neck, legs, and head by creating shallow indentations.

Texture the top of the snout by scoring the surface with a toothpick.

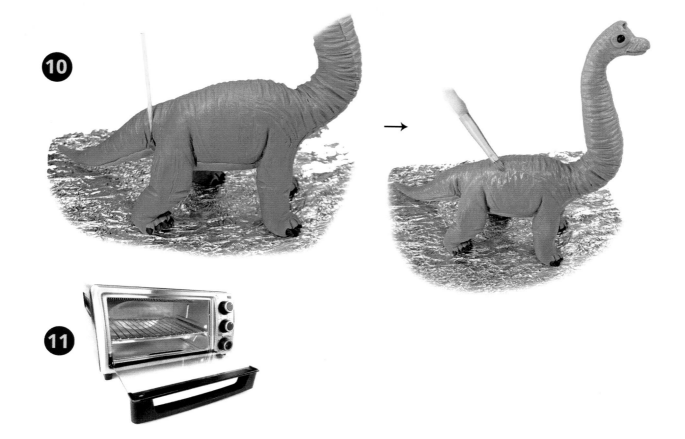

10 Texture the tail with a toothpick then smooth the surface with a brush and small amount of baby oil.

11 Bake the sculpture at 250°F for 20 minutes.

Dilophosaurus

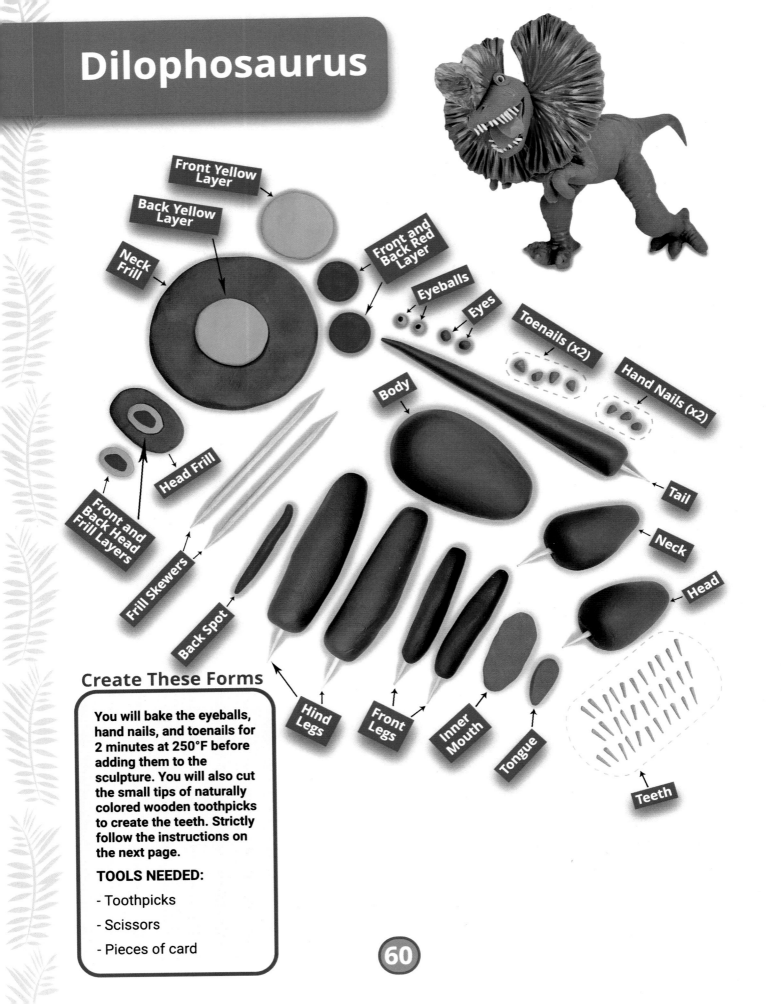

Front Yellow Layer

Back Yellow Layer

Neck Frill

Front and Back Red Layer

Eyeballs

Eyes

Toenails (x2)

Hand Nails (x2)

Body

Tail

Head Frill

Neck

Front and Back Head Frill Layers

Head

Frill Skewers

Back Spot

Hind Legs

Front Legs

Inner Mouth

Tongue

Teeth

Create These Forms

You will bake the eyeballs, hand nails, and toenails for 2 minutes at 250°F before adding them to the sculpture. You will also cut the small tips of naturally colored wooden toothpicks to create the teeth. Strictly follow the instructions on the next page.

TOOLS NEEDED:

- Toothpicks

- Scissors

- Pieces of card

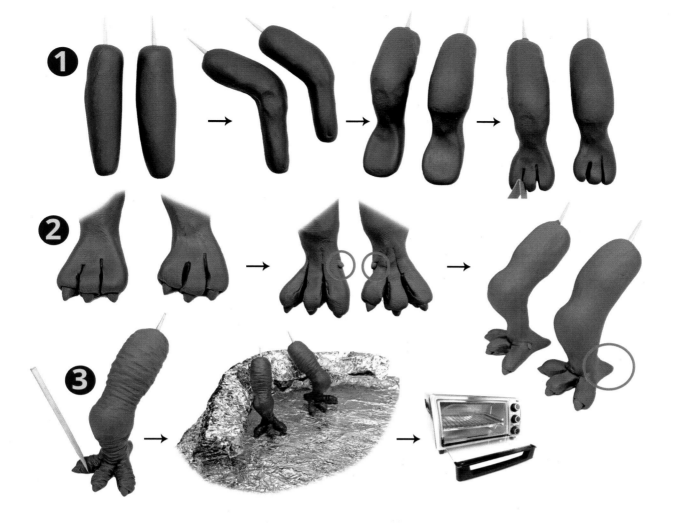

1 Prepare the skewered hind legs clay. Bend the clay and skewer at the midpoint of each leg. This will break the toothpick inside. Pinch the end tips of the legs to create the feet formations. Use a piece of folded card to slice two evenly spaced lines. This will create three toes in each foot.

2 Add the baked toenails to the tip of each toe and one nail for each dew claw.

Pinch the back of both feet to create a heel for stability.

3 Using a toothpick, texture the legs with horizontal indentations.

Place the hind legs on an aluminum platform. Smooth the surface with a brush and small amount of baby oil. Make sure that both legs are upright. Bake the sculpture at 250°F for 20 minutes.

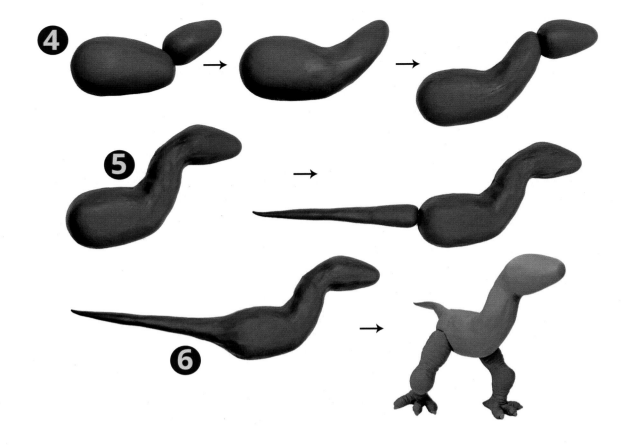

4   Attach the neck to the body then blend the connection.

Attach the head to the front tip of the neck.

5   Blend the connection between the head and neck.

Attach the tail.

6   Blend the connection between the tail and body.

After the baked hind legs cool off, attach them to the body. Blend the connections, smoothing the soft clay towards the baked clay.

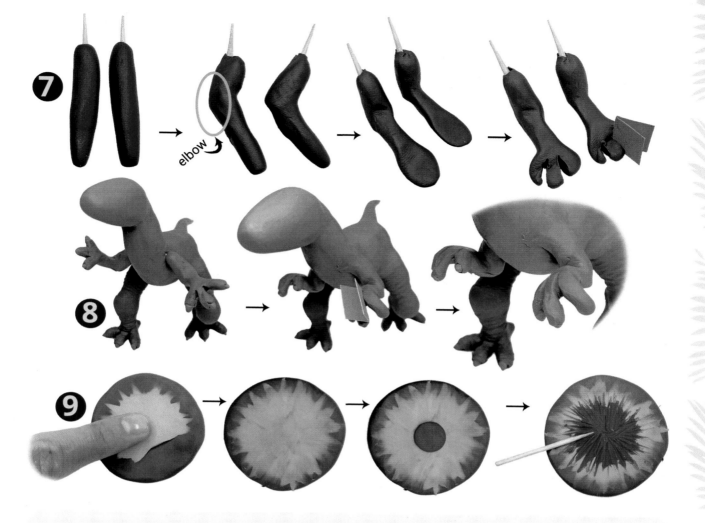

7 Prepare the skewered front legs. Bend the clay and skewer at the midpoint of each front leg. This will break the toothpick inside and create an elbow.

Pinch the end tips of the front legs to create the hand formations. Use a piece of folded card to slice two evenly spaced lines. This will create three fingers on each hand.

8 Add the baked hand nails to the tip of each finger. Use the piece of card to further define and separate the fingers.

Attach the front leg formations to each side of the shoulder area then blend the connections.

Bend each finger downward.

9 Prepare the neck frill. Using your fingertip, smear the back yellow layer into a sunburst-like shape.

Add one red layer clay to the middle of the smeared yellow layer.

Using a toothpick, spread the red layer outward by lightly scoring the clay.

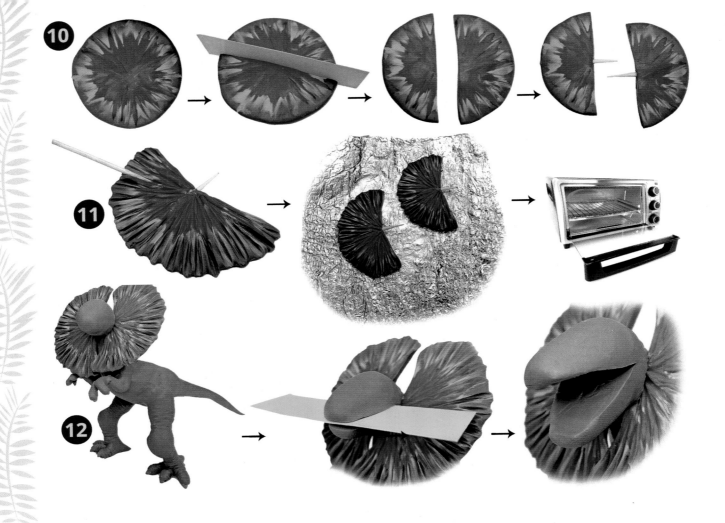

10 Using your fingertip, gently smear the scored red layer clay.

Repeat steps 9 and 10 on the other side of the neck frill.

Using a piece of card, slice the neck frill in half. Trim two toothpick skewers then insert them into the neck frill at the midpoint.

11 Texture the neck frill on both sides by scoring the clay deeply with a toothpick. Place both textured neck frills on an aluminum platform then bake at 250°F for 10 minutes.

12 After the baked frills cool off, attach a frill to each side of the neck.

Using a piece of card, deeply slice the mouth horizontally then open the mouth.

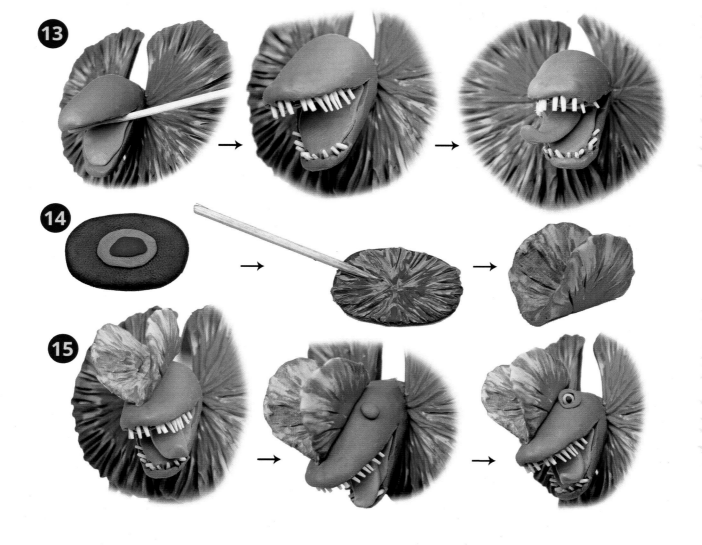

13   Use a toothpick to place the inner mouth clay inside the mouth.

Add the teeth on the inner edges of the lower and upper mouth.

Add the tongue inside the mouth.

14   Prepare the head frill. Using a toothpick, spread the yellow and red layers in a similar pattern to the neck frills. Fold the head frill into the shape of a taco.

15   Place the head frill on top of the head and lightly depress the middle with a toothpick to help the head frill adhere to the head.

Add the eyes to each side of the head.

Add and depress the baked eyeballs on the eyes.

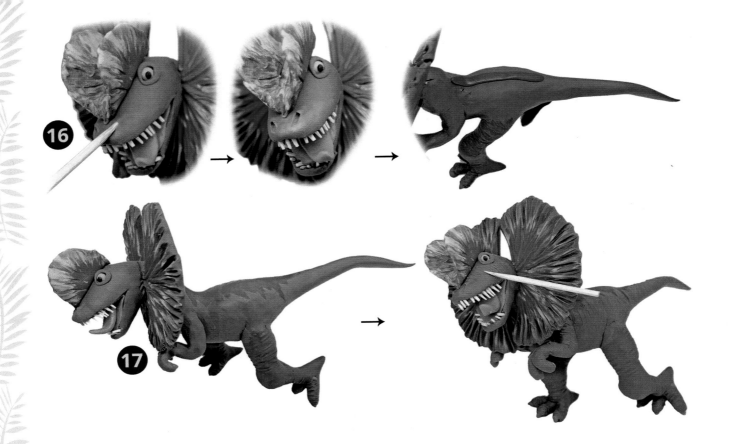

16 Using a toothpick, poke two slanted holes into the front of the snout to create nostrils.

Add the back spot, aligning it with the spine of the dinosaur.

17 Smear the sides of the back spot downwards then smear the green clay from the body upwards, creating an irregular zigzag pattern.

Texture the face, head, and front legs by scoring the clay with a toothpick.

18 Place the sculpture on an aluminum platform. Smooth the surface with a brush and small amount of baby oil.

Prop the sculpture up with balls of aluminum foil placed under the front and hind legs and tail. This will help stabilize the sculpture for baking.

19 Bake the sculpture at 250°F for 20 minutes.

Ankylosaurus

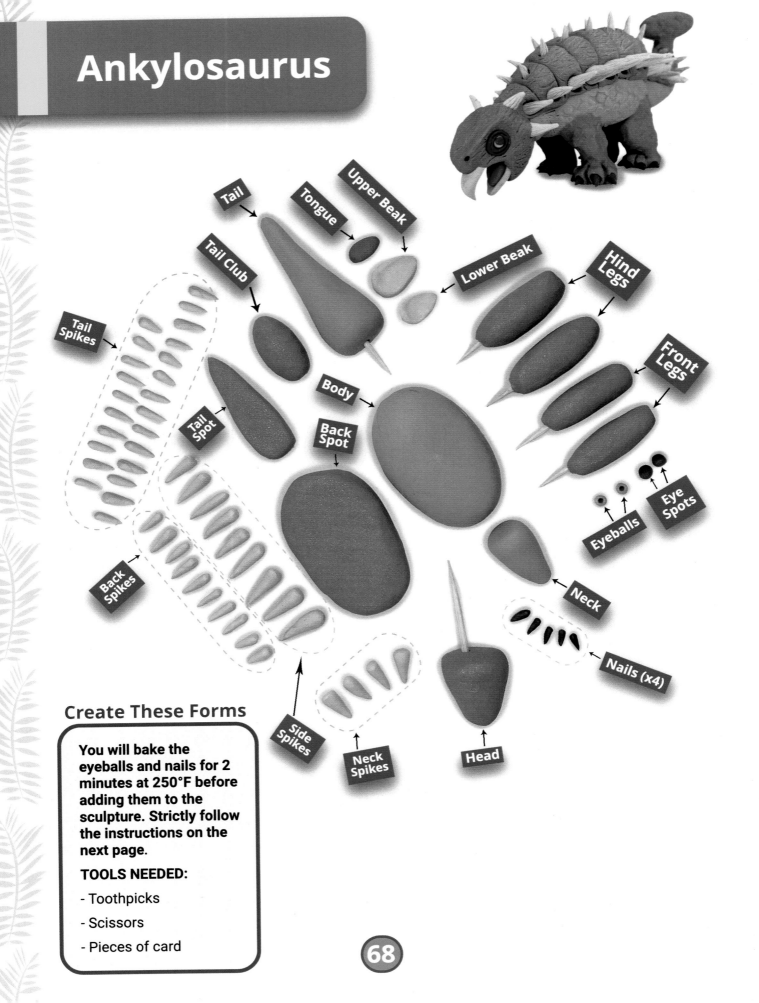

Tail

Tongue

Upper Beak

Tail Club

Lower Beak

Hind Legs

Tail Spikes

Front Legs

Body

Tail Spot

Back Spot

Eye Spots

Eyeballs

Back Spikes

Neck

Nails (x4)

Side Spikes

Neck Spikes

Head

Create These Forms

You will bake the eyeballs and nails for 2 minutes at 250°F before adding them to the sculpture. Strictly follow the instructions on the next page.

TOOLS NEEDED:

- Toothpicks

- Scissors

- Pieces of card

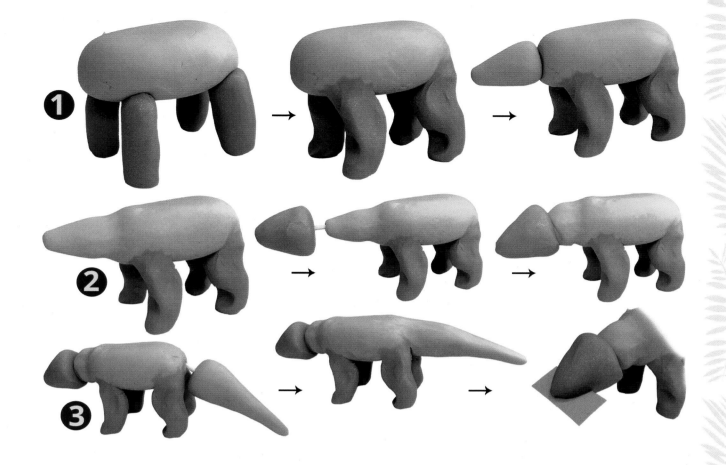

1   Attach the front and hind legs to the body then blend the connections. Lightly pinch the midpoint of each leg to create knees and elbows. Lightly pinch the endpoint of each leg to create feet.

Attach the neck.

2   Blend connection between the neck and body.

Attach the head to the front of the neck. Lightly press the head towards the neck without blending the connection.

3   Attach the tail then blend the connection.

Slice the mouth horizontally with a piece of card.

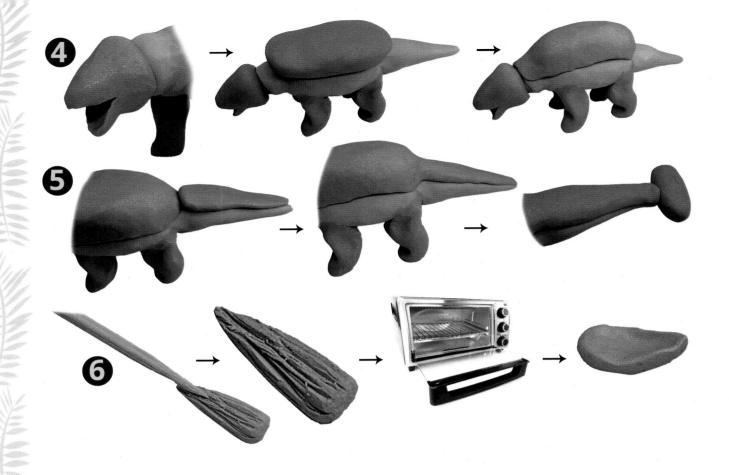

4   Open the mouth. Add the back spot on top of the body. Gently press the edges of the back spot towards the body. Create a rounded oblong shape for the back spot.

5   Add the tail spot on top of the tail then flatten the edges of the tail spot with your fingertip. Attach the tail club to the tip of the tail.

6   Using a toothpick, texture the tail, back, side, and neck spikes by scoring the clay. Bake the spikes at 250°F for 2 minutes.

Prepare the upper beak. Form the beak concave with one end pointed.

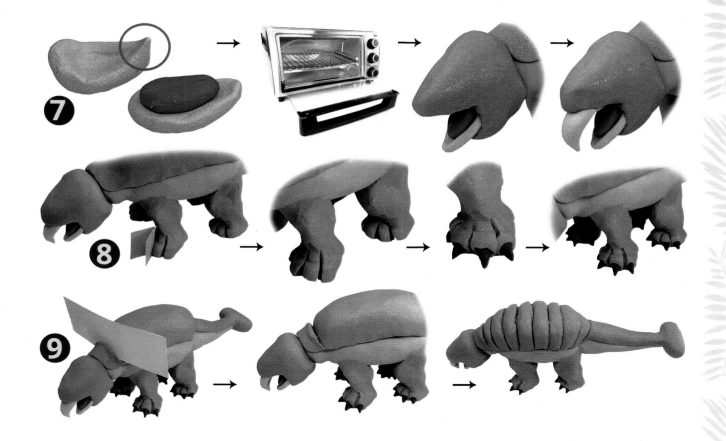

7 Make sure to form the tip of the upper beak into a sharp point. Form the lower beak into a shallow concave shape then place the tongue on top. Bake both beaks at 250°F for 2 minutes.

After the beaks cool off, first place the baked lower beak inside the lower mouth then place the baked upper beak on inner top of the mouth pointing downward.

8 Use a piece of card to slice three evenly spaced lines in the hands and feet. This will create four toes in each hand and foot.

Add the baked nails to the tip of each finger and toe.

9 Using a long piece of card, slice one horizontal line on the back neck area. Gently press the card towards the back to create a rounded edge.

Repeat this process to create 9 evenly spaced horizontal sections on the back.

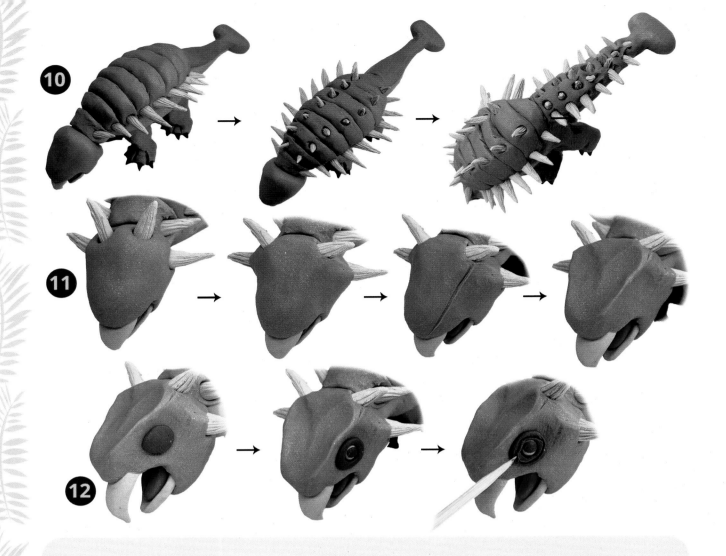

10 Insert the baked side spikes on each side of the dinosaur.

Insert the baked back spikes in two parallel lines on the upper back.

Insert the tail spikes on the upper part of the tail.

11 Insert the four neck spikes around the base of the head then lightly press the clay surrounding the spikes.

Using a toothpick, draw two parallel lines on top of the head, starting at the front snout and moving towards the forehead. Pinch the lines to create two parallel raised crests.

12 Add the eye spots to each side of the head.

Add and depress the baked eyeballs in the middle of each eye.

Score the eye around the eyeballs with a toothpick.

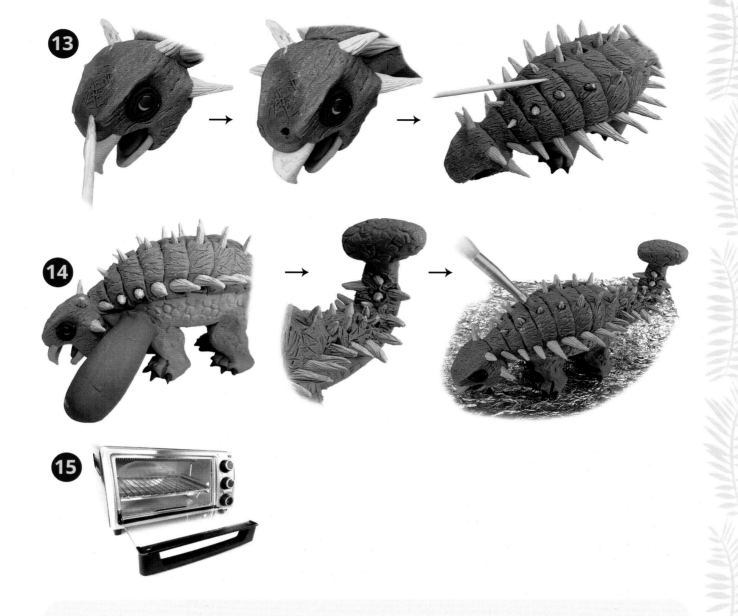

13 Using a toothpick, poke two holes in the front of the snout to create nostrils.

Texture the body, back, head, face, legs, and tail by scoring the clay with a toothpick.

14 Use your Do-It-Yourself skin texturing tool to texture the body.

Maneuver the tail to bend upwards.

Place the sculpture on an aluminum platform. Smooth the surface with a brush and small amount of baby oil.

15 Bake the sculpture at 250°F for 20 minutes.

Triceratops

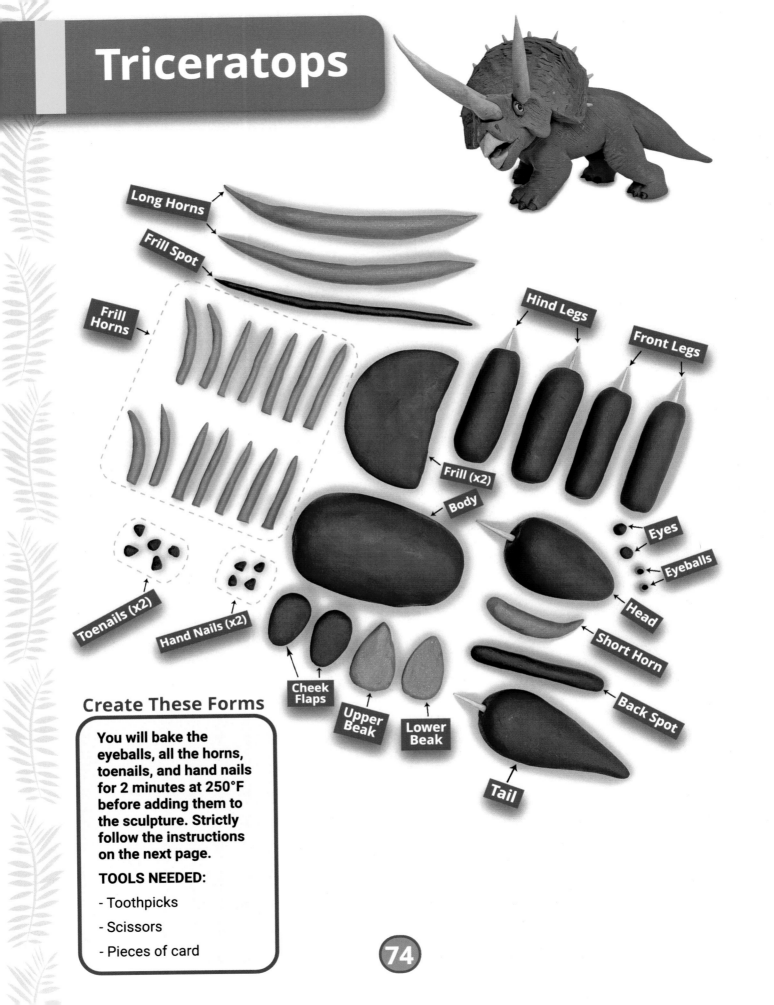

Long Horns

Frill Spot

Frill Horns

Hind Legs

Front Legs

Frill (x2)

Body

Eyes

Eyeballs

Head

Short Horn

Back Spot

Toenails (x2)

Hand Nails (x2)

Cheek Flaps

Upper Beak

Lower Beak

Tail

Create These Forms

You will bake the eyeballs, all the horns, toenails, and hand nails for 2 minutes at 250°F before adding them to the sculpture. Strictly follow the instructions on the next page.

TOOLS NEEDED:

- Toothpicks

- Scissors

- Pieces of card

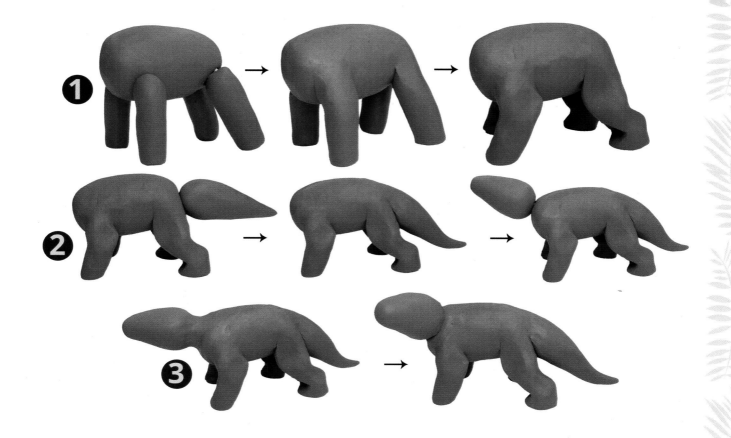

1   Attach the front and hind legs to the body then blend the connections. Lightly pinch the midpoint of each leg to create knees and elbows. Lightly pinch the endpoint of each leg to create hands and feet.

2   Attach the tail then blend the connection.

       Attach the neck.

3   Blend the connection between the neck and head.

       Maneuver the head to face slightly sideways.

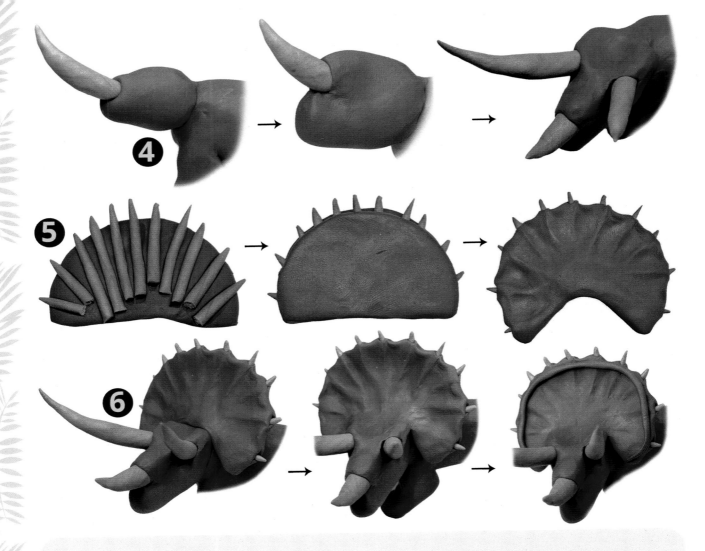

4 Insert the baked short horn in the middle of the head. Make sure that front tip of the horn is pointing upward. Depress the horn until about half its length is inside the forehead. Lightly press the clay surrounding the horn and form a snout under the horn.

Insert the two baked long horns on each side of the forehead pointing forward and up.

5 Prepare the frill and the baked frill horns. Arrange the frill horns on top of the frill in a fan-like formation and pointing outward.

Place the second frill on top of the frill horns then lightly press the clay. The outline of frill horns underneath the clay will be visible.

6 Place the new frill formation on top of the head then blend the connection at the forehead. Place the frill spot on the front edge of the frill.

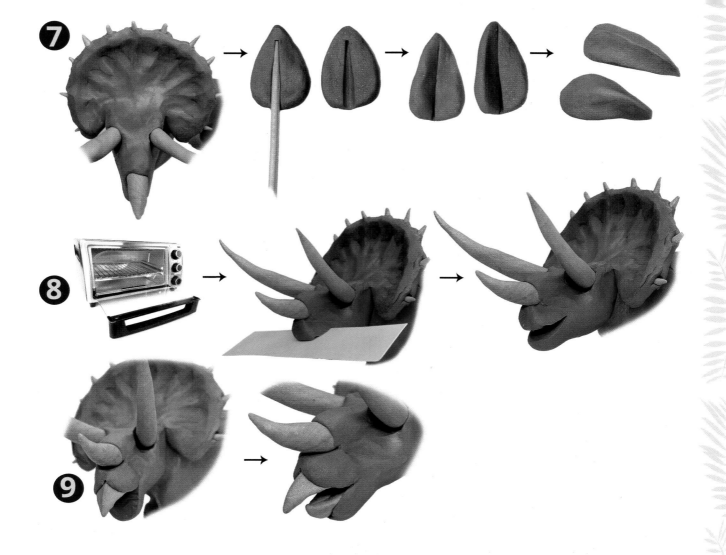

7 Using your fingertip, smear the frill spot clay downward on the frill.

Prepare the upper and lower beak. Create an indentation on each beak with a toothpick then slightly fold the beaks towards the midline. Turn the beaks over then pinch the middle of each beak to create a raised line.

8 Bake the beaks at 250°F for 2 minutes.

Slice the mouth horizontally with a piece of card then open the mouth.

9 After the baked beaks cool off, place the upper beak on the inner part of the upper mouth pointing downwards. Place the baked lower beak on the inner part of the lower mouth pointing upwards. Make sure that the lower beak is shorter than the upper beak.

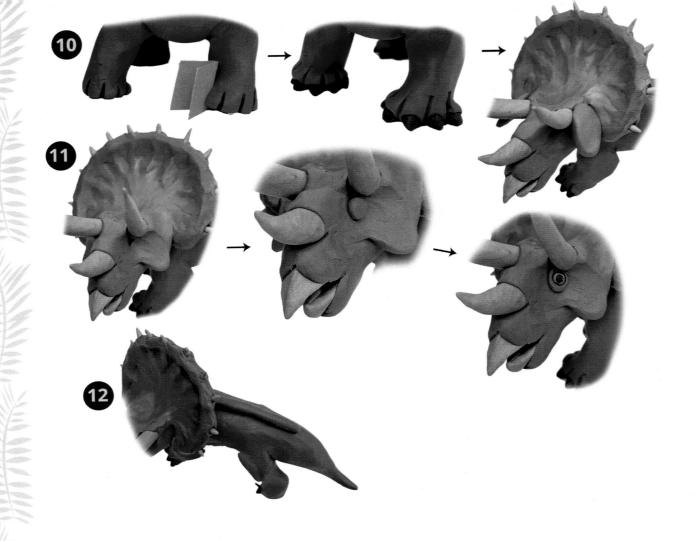

10 Use a piece of folded card to slice four evenly spaced lines on the hands and feet. This will create five toes in each hand and foot.

Add the baked nails to the tip of each finger and toe.

Place the cheek flaps on the sides of the head right next to the long horns and pointing downward.

11 Blend the connection between the cheek flaps and face.

Add the eyes right below the long horns.

Add and depress the baked eyeballs in each eye.

12 Add the back spot, aligning it with the spine of the dinosaur.

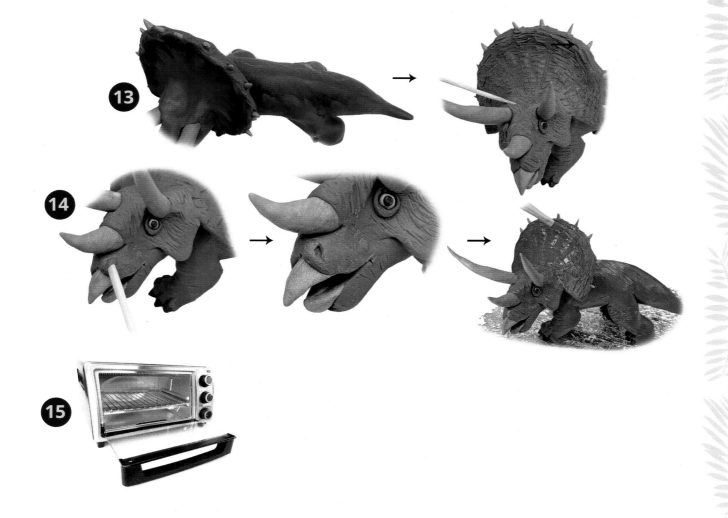

13 Smear the sides of the back spot downwards then smear the red clay from the body upwards.

Using a toothpick, texture the head, frill, face, tail, and legs by scoring the clay.

14 Using a toothpick, poke two holes in the front of the snout to form nostrils.

Smooth the surface with a brush and small amount of baby oil.

15 Bake the sculpture at 250°F for 20 minutes.

Stegosaurus

Tail Spikes

Belly Spot

Tail Spot

Body

Back Plates

Tail

Neck

Head

Eyeballs

Hind Legs

Front Legs

Create These Forms

You will bake the eyeballs and tail spikes for 2 minutes at 250°F before adding them to the sculpture. Strictly follow the instructions on the next page.

TOOLS NEEDED:

- Toothpicks

- Scissors

- Pieces of card

-Sculpey Oven-Bake Clay Adhesive

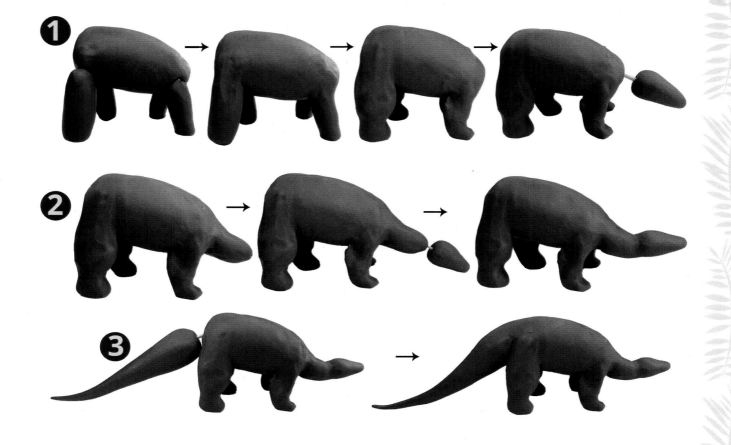

1   Attach the front and hind legs to the body then blend the connections. Lightly pinch the midpoint of each leg to create knees and elbows. Lightly pinch the endpoint of each leg to create hands and feet.

Attach the neck.

2   Blend the connection between the neck and body.

Attach the head to the front of the neck then blend the connection.

3   Attach the tail then blend the connection.

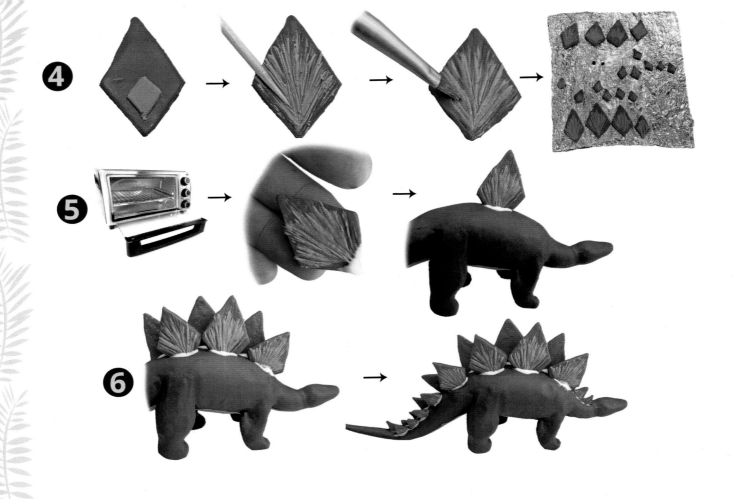

4 Prepare the back plates. Spread the yellow clay outwards towards the edges of the plates by scoring with a toothpick. Smooth the scored clay with a brush and small amount of baby oil. Repeat this process for all the other back plates. Place the back plates on an aluminum platform.

5 Bake the back plates at 250°F for 2 minutes.

After the bake plates cool off, apply a small amount of Sculpey Oven-Bake Clay Adhesive liquid at the bottom tip of the biggest back plate then attach it to the mid-back, aligning the plate with the spine of the dinosaur.

6 Repeat this process to secure the remaining back plates to the back of the dinosaur.

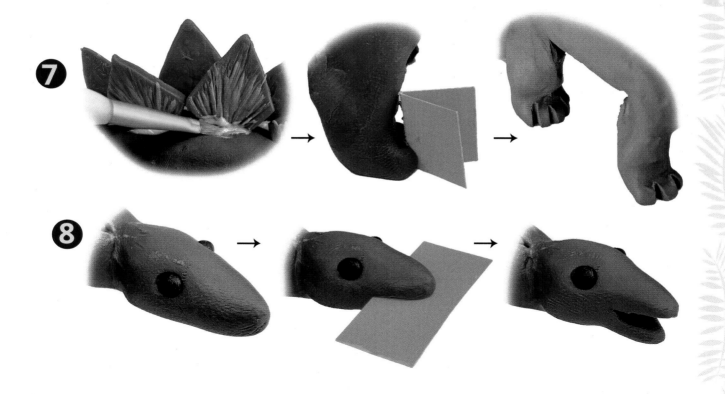

7 Remove and spread any excess adhesive liquid with a brush.

Use a folded piece of card to slice two evenly spaced lines in both hands. This will create three fingers for each hand. Use a card to slide four evenly spaced lines in both feet. This will create five toes on each foot.

8 Place the baked eyeballs on each side of the head.

Slice the mouth horizontally with a piece of card then open the mouth.

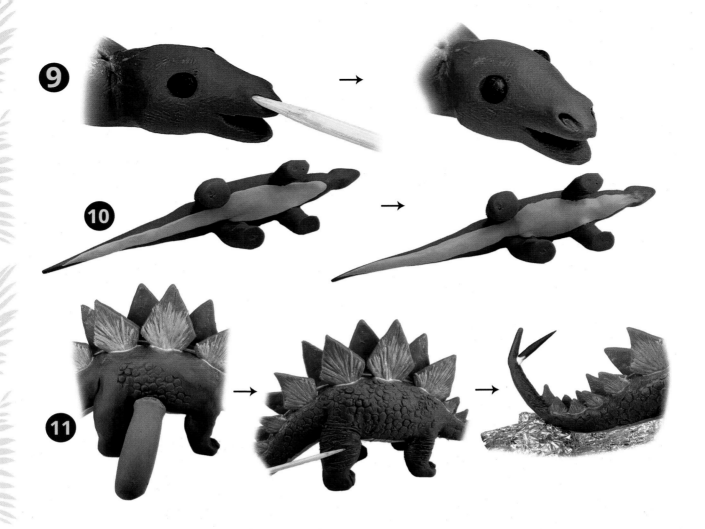

9   Using a toothpick, poke two slanted holes in the front of the snout to create nostrils.

10   Place the belly spot along the belly area and the tail spot along the bottom tail area. Lightly press and flatten the edges of the spots with your fingertip.

11   Use your Do-It-Yourself skin texturing tool to texture the body. Texture the legs with a toothpick by scoring the clay.

Place the sculpture on an aluminum platform.

Maneuver the tail upward.

Apply a small amount of Sculpey Oven-Bake Clay Adhesive liquid on the bottom tip of a baked tail spike then attach it to the tip of the tail pointing forward.

12 Repeat this process to attach the rest of the baked tail spikes to the tip of the tail.

Using a toothpick, texture the head and face by scoring the clay.

13 Smooth the surface with a brush and small amount of baby oil.

Bake the sculpture at 250°F for 20 minutes.

A MESSAGE FROM THE ARTIST

Hello to all who have a copy of *DOGGO BAKE For Beginners! BOOK ONE, DOGGO BAKE For Beginners! BOOK TWO, DIY Realistic Dog Sculptures 1 (French Bulldog Edition),* or any other JFCRN book! We would love to see your creations!

Please use the hashtag #ImadeitJFCRN on social media and tag your dog sculpture projects so that we can inspire others.

Thank you so much!